LOST DEARBORN

LOST DEARBORN

CRAIG E. HUTCHISON

THE History PRESS

Published by The History Press
Charleston, SC
www.historypress.net

Front cover: The Ford Rotunda as it appeared in 1958. In 1935–36, Henry Ford had the main structure moved from the grounds of the Chicago World's Fair and placed across from the Ford Motor Company's Administration building on Schaefer Road. At the time, it was the largest permanent industrial exhibit building in the country and became one of the top tourist attractions during the 1950s and early 1960s.

First published 2017

Manufactured in the United States

ISBN 9781467136266

Library of Congress Control Number: 2017953986

DEDICATION

To those who have played a huge role in my life, my parents, my wife and several teachers whom I am sure had no idea of the impact they were making on my path at the time. I could never fully express my gratitude to these individuals. To Jack Tate, I am thankful that I met you. You not only served as an excellent boss from whom I learned a tremendous amount, but I also now count you as a good friend and that is a treasure indeed. And to my girls, Abigail and Lydia, you have changed my world in ways I don't even understand, but I thank God for you and I look forward to growing together and making this a wonderful life.

CONTENTS

ACKNOWLEDGEMENTS

This book would never have seen the light of day without the assistance and support of Jack Tate, the acting chief curator of the Dearborn Historical Museum. Not only did Jack allow and assist with the much-needed research, he also allowed me to tap into his extensive knowledge of the Dearborn area, for which I will be forever grateful. No matter how far removed I get from my undergraduate days at the University of Michigan, this section would not be complete, and in fact, the story of my life cannot be fully and adequately told without mentioning Dr. Martin Hershock and Dr. Gerry Moran. I am a very blessed man to have studied historical topics under these two amazing scholars, and the passion, skills and knowledge they instilled in me have stayed with me until this day. They have inspired me to stay true to my passion. They taught me how to look at history from different viewpoints—what a special thing to impart. Dr. Donn Werling is another influence in my life who deserves mention. His love of historical interpretation and how it can play out in the lives of the public continues to serve as an inspiration to me when working on projects like this. His combination of passion, love and knowledge has served as an inspiration that I know will always be with me. And he has always been an encouragement and an example of not only dreaming big but also finding ways to make dreams a reality. And thank you to my wife and my girls for letting me sneak in the hours needed for this project. I hope I am able to instill in Abigail and Lydia a love of history like I have always had. Finally, I would like to thank those who will read this publication. I truly hope that these pages bring to life the rich history that has flowed through the Dearborn area and that you leave this book with an appreciation for what has come before us and for what makes Dearborn such a fascinating place. Those of us who have grown up here have been blessed people; sometimes I think we forget that. May this serve as a reminder.

INTRODUCTION

It is not uncommon for residents of an area to be completely unaware of the interesting and rich history that led to the present. What exists today did not just happen overnight. Someone at some point in time built the foundation. All around are familiar streets, buildings and tracts of land. But what are they rooted to? Where did they come from? And even for current or former residents who do have memories of significant events or structures or people, sometimes life can certainly begin to get in the way of those memories. It is for all of these reasons that this book was created. Dearborn, for its size, has too interesting a tale to tell not to keep the stories and memories alive. And many of the great stories of Dearborn are rooted in structures that became significant to area residents over time and during specific eras. And one thing Dearborn has certainly had over its history are many unique eras.

The seal of the City of Dearborn denotes that the area was settled in 1786. This may have been true of the first European settlers, who were of French descent. But for hundreds of years prior to the arrival of the French, Native Americans traveled by canoe up and down the Rouge River. Woodland tribes, including the Ottawa, Potawatomi, Saux-Fox and Chippewa, never permanently settled here but they camped along the banks of the Rouge, which at the time was clean and clear and teeming with fish. The Rouge River provided access to the interior of the land. To travel by land, there was an Indian trail known as the Great Sauk Trail (today Michigan Avenue). This trail was also used by French explorers, fur traders and missionaries.

The early French settlers established "ribbon farms," which were narrow strips of land that fronted the river while the rest of the farm extended into the forest. This gave everyone access to the river for the growing of crops and provided access to the markets in Detroit via water.

The early settlers were mainly concerned about one thing: survival. And survival meant providing for shelter, food, water and clothing. Early in the area's history, a person couldn't just run up to the corner store to obtain these necessities. The early settlers had to literally cut out an existence on what was then considered the frontier. The opening of the Erie Canal in 1825 as well as the coming of the railroad brought more settlers and more opportunity. The canal reduced a five- to ten-day arduous land journey to a forty-four-hour water route. Traveling by land in these early days was very difficult, as there were few roads and those that did exist were in very poor condition. For a moment, imagine the life of those early pioneers as they arrived at a tract of land that would need to be transformed into a farm. But when looking around, these early settlers were faced with a major problem: there were trees everywhere one looked. William Nowlin was a descendant of one of these early families, and he stated in the strongest terms what the landscape meant to anyone who desired to stay: "The forest meant very hard work for the settler: so much that nowadays one is apt to wonder how on earth any of them accomplished it."

Being chosen as the location for the new U.S. Arsenal created a focal point, and its impact on this area cannot be overstated. The building of the arsenal attracted many different types of skilled workers. Brickmaking became an important industry. Much of the area's soil is composed of a clay material that turned out to be perfect for the making of bricks, which was actually the first industry that the area became famous for.

As the 1800s were coming to a close, Henry Ford and industrialization were looming at the door. In a very short amount of time, an area that had fewer than five thousand people ballooned to more than fifty thousand. Steady work and decent pay attracted people from everywhere it seemed. And with progress there were new structures built to fill a need or, in some cases, a desire. At the beginning, needs were more on the simple side. Taverns and general stores providing for the necessities of life were built on the main thoroughfare. As more people came, new schools sprouted up, homes were being built at a record pace, beautiful theaters were erected and the area was off and running. The pages that follow discuss and depict the past, what used to exist. And with such a rich history, these places deserve to be remembered. Most of the actual places are long-gone now.

But every single one is a part of Dearborn's great foundation, development and its very existence.

It is not often talked about, but the lives of human beings revolve around buildings of all sorts. Various structures that have been built during the stages of a community's growth provide places for people to live, conduct business, administer leadership, entertain, educate and any number of additional endeavors that men and women find a need or a desire to do. The Dearborn area followed the pattern of most settlements in that one of the earliest needs was building material. Wood was in great demand and by virtue of that requirement, sawmills were needed. As more settlers came into the area, the needs increased and the buildings that would fill those needs began to be constructed. General stores, dry goods stores, clothing stores, hardware stores, banks, schools and churches were built. Many would call these structures the lifeblood of a community. Whatever was called for or needed, Dearborn has had at one time or another.

As the area became more settled, additional development brought the people of Dearborn every imaginable business and attraction—to the point where residents would not even have to step outside of the borders to obtain what they needed. These structures and the people who owned them and ran them deserve to be remembered for the foundation they created and maintained through the years. Read the following pages with the understanding that not every development or structure that has ever existed in Dearborn is shown or written about here. Restrictions in terms of time and space prohibit such a publication. For every site discussed here, there will be several others that come to mind in the same genre. In fact, three or four books just like this could be filled with the wide variety of operations that have served area residents. The locations on these pages have been chosen to provide a representative sample in understanding what has been and—at the same time—to highlight some truly unique places that have served those who visited them. There is something that exists in all of us that yearns to make a connection with the past. As Freeman Tilden states in *Interpreting Our Heritage*, it is when this connection is made that a person "is lifted beyond and above himself into higher worlds where he talks with all his great ancestors, one of an illustrious group whose blood is in his veins and whose domain and reputation he proudly bears." The goal of this publication is to help those who read it make those connections and to appreciate what has gone on before the present day in the making of a foundation for those who call this home today.

1

THE ARSENAL'S WALLS HAVE FALLEN

One of the most important events to ever happen to the Dearborn area was its selection in 1832 by the federal government as the site for the building of a United States Arsenal. Historians have proposed three reasons as to why the arsenal was built in what was then a community by the name of Dearbornville. Some historians have proposed that the selection had something to do with potential migration of new settlers from the east and possible problems with Native Americans in the old Northwest Territory. It has also been suggested that Lewis Cass, who in 1832 was the secretary of war and had served as the first territorial governor, had something to do with its placement because of his ties to the area. And still others have argued that the Detroit Arsenal was simply moved west to protect the growing population in Detroit from the explosive materials that the arsenal housed.

Whatever the reason or reasons may have been for its placement, the decision transformed the area from a farming center to a mixture of farming, industry and military. The work of building the facility attracted locals and those from other areas who could engage in the occupations of brickmaker or tradesman. The 1839 *Gazetteer of the State of Michigan* contains an apt description of how the complex was organized and of the surrounding community, as well as the buildings that were erected and the function they would serve:

> *Dearbornville, a village and post office in the township of Dearborn and county of Wayne, situated on the south branch of the Rouge, eight miles (by land) from its mouth, 28-1/2 miles from Monroe, and 10 from Detroit. Here is a church for Methodists, erected, a saw mill with double saws, flour mill, with two run of stones, 7 stores, 2 smitheries, and a foundry for iron, propelled by horse power, a physician, and about 60 families. It is passed by the Chicago Road and State Road to Monroe, and by the Detroit and St. Joseph railroad, which has a depot or station at this point. Dearbornville is a flourishing village. Here is located the United State Arsenal. This was commenced in 1833 and completed in 1837. It consists of eleven buildings, built of brick, arranged around a square, whose side is 360 feet. The principle building occupies the center of the eastern side of the square, and is 120 feet long by 30 deep, and three stories high exclusive of the basement. This is intended for the depot of arms. The buildings surrounding this square are connected by a continuous wall of heavy masonry, 12 feet high, all calculated as a defense against an invading or insurrectionary foe. The buildings are calculated to accommodate two officers and 50 artificers and workmen and in case of emergency, they can easily accommodate double that number. The whole object of this institution is not a military station of soldiers, but for the mounting and equipping of artillery; repairing small arms, and the preparation of all the other numerous munitions of war. It is intended more particularly for the supply of Michigan and Wisconsin, in time of war, and to issue to both, in time of peace, such arms and equipment as each State, by the Acts of Congress, are thereunto entitled.*

The main function of the arsenal was to store, develop, manufacture, test, repair and provide arms and ammunition to what was then known as the western frontier. During the Civil War, it was used as a training center for recruits and as a rendezvous point to muster soldiers to the South. The Detroit Arsenal at Dearbornville operated for forty-two years, until 1875, when Congress decided it was no longer useful. At that point, it passed into the hands of the Interior Department and was subdivided into lots and the land and buildings sold.

During its operation, the eleven buildings of the arsenal each had a unique purpose. In 1832, Lieutenant Joshua Howard, serving at the present arsenal—which was down in Detroit on Jefferson Avenue—was given the responsibility of building the new installation. Much of the building materials arrived via steam ferry traveling up the Rouge River from the Detroit River. At first, Howard found navigation of the Rouge to be extremely difficult, and he spent $300 to improve the river. An additional $200 was spent to make improvements to the road that led from the boat landing to the arsenal site.

In 1833, construction began on the first building, the armory. When the cornerstone was laid, it contained a silver plate with a long inscription, which read, in part, "The site of this Arsenal was determined in 1832, Michigan being then a Territory and this spot a wilderness. The grounds were prepared in the Spring of 1833 and the cornerstone was laid the 30th of July the same year." The plate also mentions well-known names to the people of the area that can still be seen and heard today. These are names that appear on street signs, buildings and as the namesake for schools, cities and counties: Major General Alexander Macomb, Honorable Lewis Cass and General Andrew Jackson. In two months, forty-five tons of stone were transported to the arsenal site as a foundation for the armory. Two area brickmakers, Titus Dort and John Cahoon, supplied thousands of bricks for

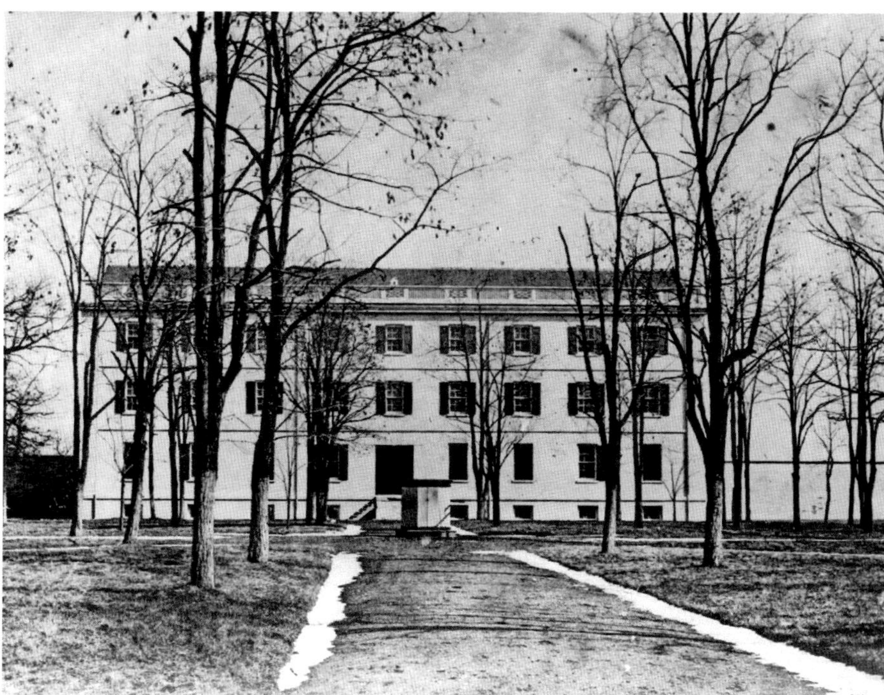

The largest of the arsenal structures, the armory was used to store ordnance equipment and quartermaster supplies. After the arsenal closed, it served as a civic center and, in 1899, was converted into the Arna Woolen Mills. A fire destroyed the structure in 1910. *Dearborn Historical Museum.*

the construction of all of the arsenal structures. In addition to brickmakers, stonemasons and carpenters were also hired for the tasks that needed to be completed. And because of its durability, slate was brought in from New York to be used for the roof of each structure. The arsenal buildings were the first structures in Michigan to have slate roofs.

The armory was the largest of all of the arsenal buildings and served as a storehouse for ordnance equipment and quartermaster supplies. The armory also served as a social center for military and community events. Around the year 1877, after the building had ceased to be an armory and the arsenal had closed, the building was converted into a community civic center called Liberty Hall. Activities such as dancing, roller skating, dramatic plays, lodge meetings and other functions were held there, and the structure had become important to the area's population as a community center. Then, in 1899, the building was converted into Arna Woolen Mills, a plant that made coats and robes. A fire caused by a lightning strike destroyed the 120-foot structure beyond repair in 1910. Residents that were present at the time of the fire claimed that the fire burned and smoldered for about twenty days. Six homes were constructed from the salvaged bricks on Garrison Street near Monroe Street and three of these homes still stand today. After the fire, the last owner of the building, Herman Kalmbach, came upon the silver plate placed in the cornerstone mentioned earlier. The plate remained in his family until 1975, when it was donated to the Dearborn Historical Museum. In 1964, the Dearborn Historical Museum excavated a portion of the foundation and unearthed artifacts; they can be viewed at the museum.

The sutler's shop was an early post exchange where personal items such as toiletries were sold to the arsenal soldiers. The shop was the equivalent of today's army post exchange. In the early days, each army installation was regularly visited by a sutler, a man who traveled from post to post with an inventory of supplies that soldiers could purchase, such as soap, toothpaste, shaving cream, candy, tobacco, sewing kits, towels, stationery and even trinkets to send home. This was a very popular place on payday. The structure still stands today, but it has been altered. After the arsenal was closed and the buildings were put up for auction, it was used as a private residence and is now used as part of a doctor's clinic on the northeast corner of Garrison Street and Monroe Street. Little is known about the guard house, the enlisted men's barracks and the surgeon's quarters. It is known that during the years following the closing of the arsenal, they were each used as residences. But all three were razed in 1892 for the erection of the Dearborn Public School.

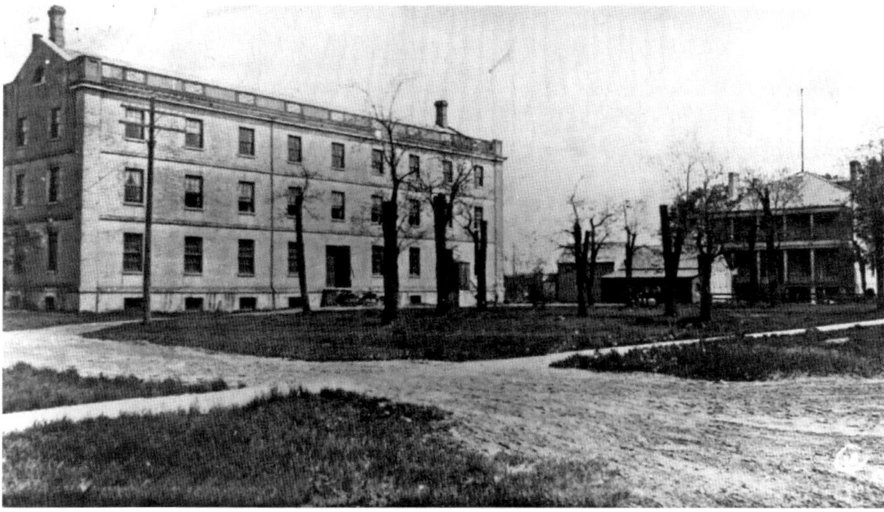

Here are two former arsenal structures pictured in 1902, the armory and the commandant's quarters. By this time, the Arna Woolen Mills Company had converted the armory to a production company where imitation buffalo robes and blankets were made. *Dearborn Historical Museum.*

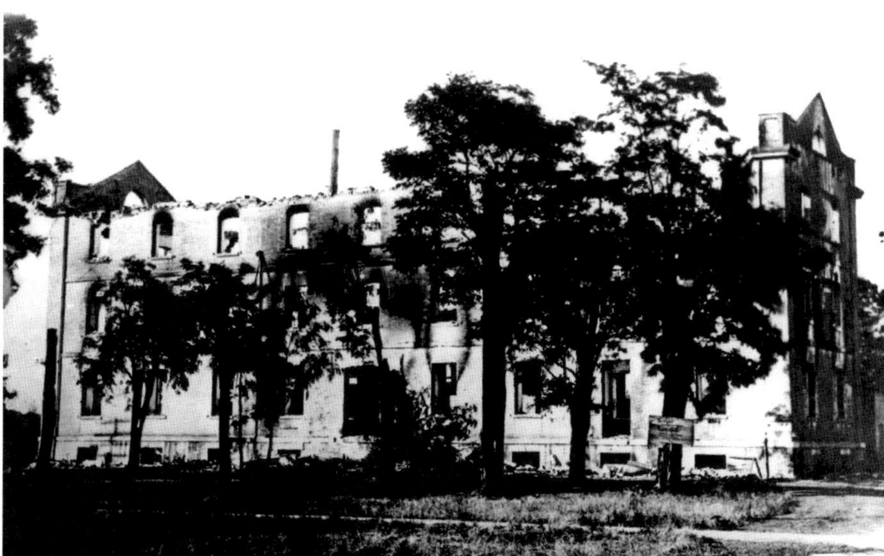

What had become the Arna Woolen Mills (served as the armory during its arsenal days) was struck by lightning and destroyed in 1910. *Dearborn Historical Museum.*

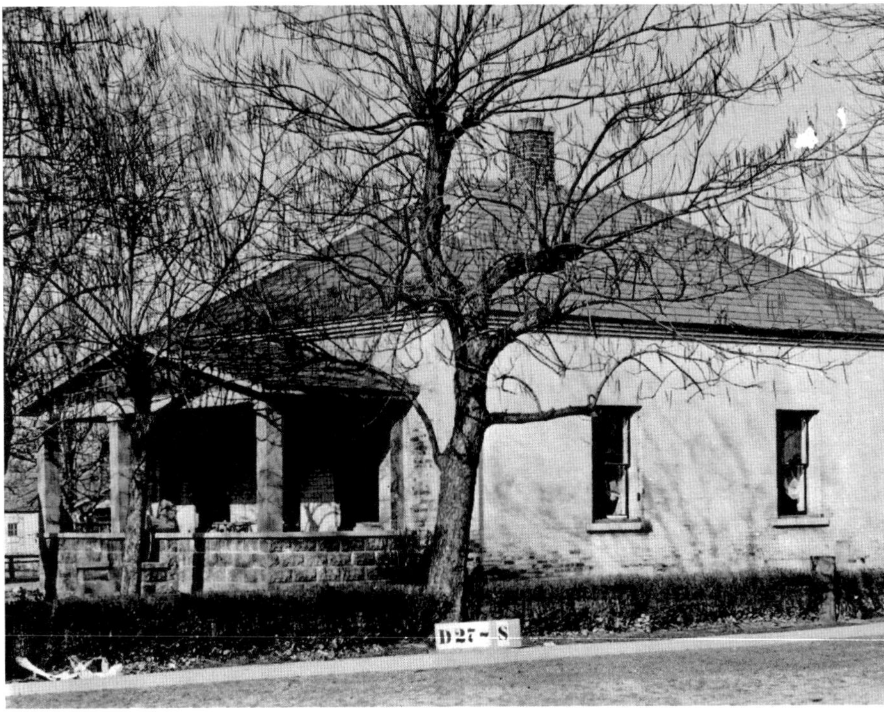

The sutler's shop served as the post exchange where personal items like toiletries were sold to arsenal soldiers. Pictured here in 1934, the structure served as a private residence for awhile. It still stands today, albeit in an altered state as part of a doctor's office. *Dearborn Historical Museum.*

By the summer of 1833, Dort had built a kiln on the arsenal premises, making it much more convenient to supply bricks for the remaining structures that needed to be built. By November of that year, Dort was making bricks to be used in the building of the officers' quarters (later known as the commandant's quarters) the next spring. The commandant's quarters served as home to nineteen commandants during its time of service. Colonel Joshua Howard, who had a long and distinguished military career, was not only the officer in charge when the arsenal was under construction, but he was also appointed the first commandant of the facility. The structure served as a center of social and cultural activities in the area until 1875. After the arsenal closed, the structure was used in a number of capacities: a multi-unit dwelling, a jail, a courthouse, the first local library, township and city offices, a school, church activities and a police station. In 1950, the building was dedicated as the City of Dearborn's first historical museum. Today, sitting

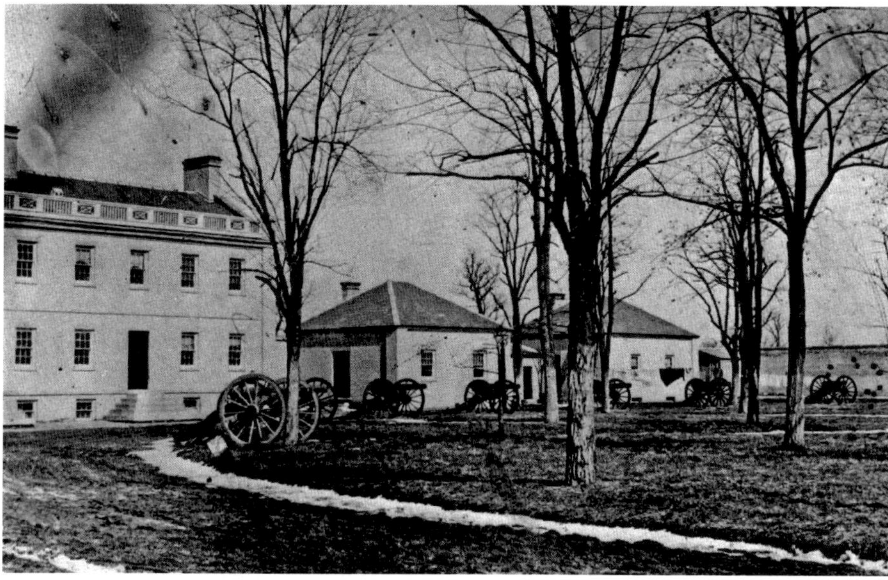

Shown from left to right in 1868 are the barracks, the guard house and the sutler's shop. The barracks and the guard house were razed to make room for a school that was built at the corner of Garrison and Monroe Streets. *Dearborn Historical Museum.*

prominently at Michigan Avenue and Monroe Street, it holds the distinction of being the oldest building in Dearborn still standing on its original site. It is still a museum today and is open to the public. It has undergone several restorations and is used to teach visitors what life was like in the area in the mid-nineteenth century. There are a number of period rooms where visitors can get a better feel for a bygone era. The State of Michigan considers this structure to be one of the seven most significant buildings in the state, and it is listed in the National Register of Historic Places.

The structure that served as the arsenal office stood very close to the commandant's quarters, and after the complex closed, it was used as a residence and a harness maker's shop by Herman Blankertz. His business began in 1894. Blankertz then purchased an old feed shop and moved his operations to 22064 Michigan Avenue in the early 1900s when the building that had served as the arsenal office, his home and harness shop was torn down to extend Monroe Street north from Michigan Avenue.

In the 1880s, a two-story structure was erected between what had been the carpenter's and blacksmith's shops. It was used as a lumber mill, a canning company, an auto repair company, the Detroit-Dearborn Motor Car Company, a machine shop and a paint shop. Of particular interest was

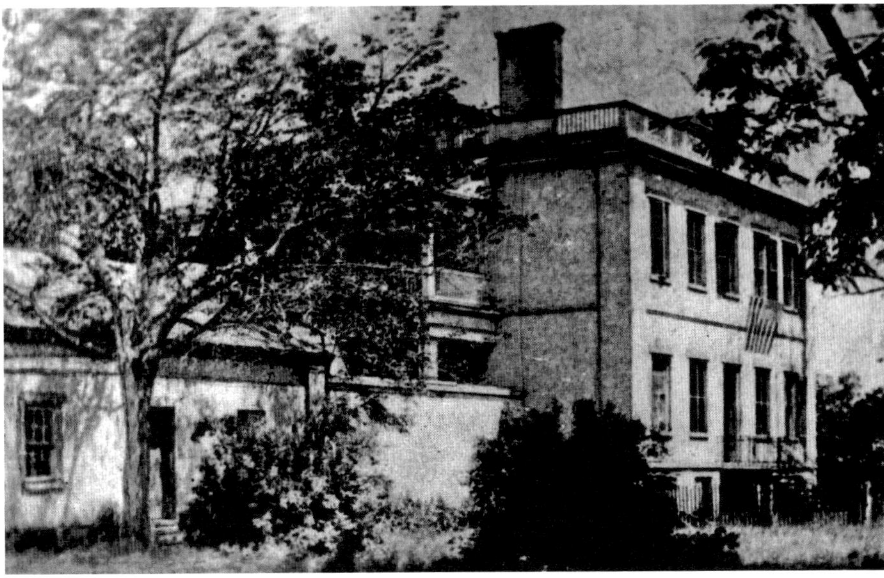

The arsenal office (*left*) and commandant's quarters (*right*) as they looked in 1890. After the arsenal closed, the house was used as a multi-person dwelling, a jail, a courthouse, the first local library, township and city offices, a school, church activities and a police station. Today, it tells the story of the arsenal and about life in the area. *Dearborn Historical Museum.*

the establishment of the Detroit-Dearborn Motor Car Company in 1909. History has shown that long-lasting success in the automobile industry has been limited to only a handful of companies. Nine investors risked a small fortune on the first automobile company in Dearborn. The company's emblem was red, white and blue, and the slogan was "Cars of Class." In terms of creating models for the company, two designs were developed, including a two-door touring roadster called the Nike and a four-door touring torpedo called the Minerva. The former blacksmith and carpenter shops of the arsenal were used to set up a main office and factory. Within a year, the first automobile was completed, giving the Detroit-Dearborn Motor Car Company the distinction of having produced the first automobile in Dearborn, seventeen years before Ford Motor Company. In the end, 110 vehicles were produced, but due to mounting debt and mismanagement of the company's resources and supplies, it went out of business. Today, this entire structure has been lost to history, as the buildings were razed in 1946. The bricks were purchased by Andy Palmer to build what became a very popular establishment known as Andy Palmer's Military Inn, which was located at Telegraph and Warren.

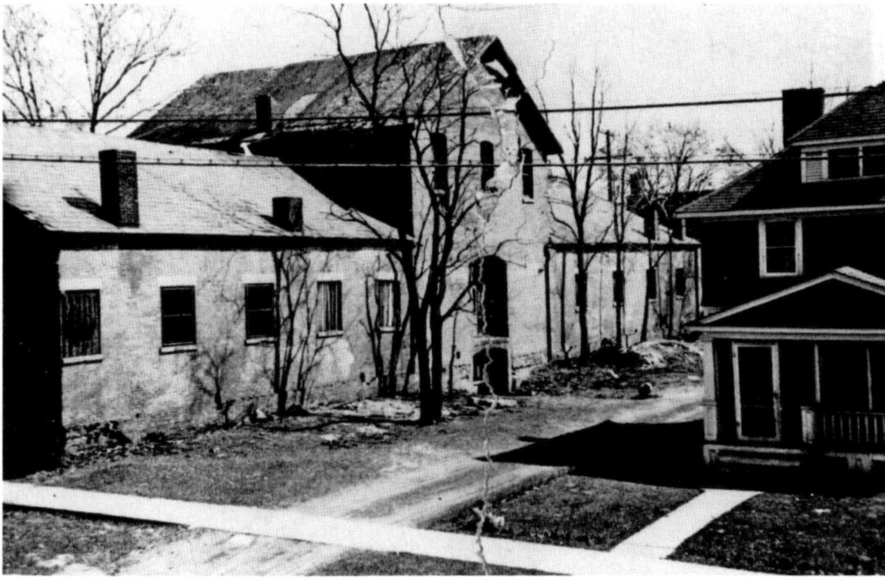

In the 1880s, a two-story structure was erected between what had been the carpenter's (*left*) and blacksmith's (*right*) shops. The complex served a number of purposes including the production of cars until it was torn down in 1946. *Dearborn Historical Museum.*

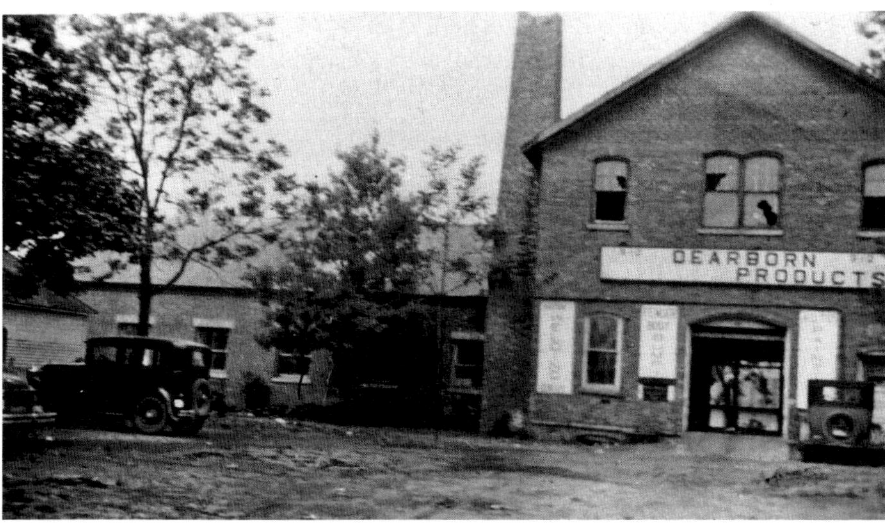

A complex that was made up of two of the old arsenal buildings (carpenter's and blacksmith's shops) and a third that was erected between the two became an auto repair business in the 1930s. *Dearborn Historical Museum.*

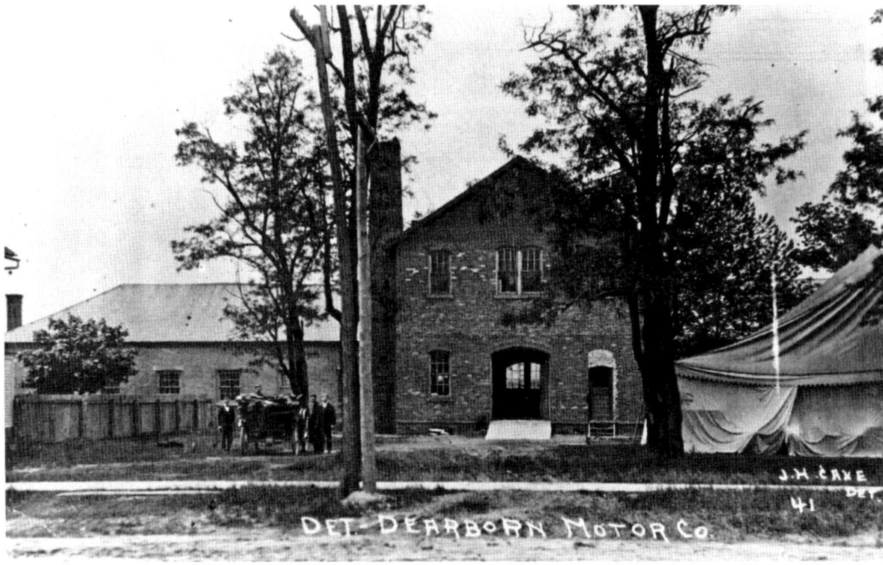

The Detroit-Dearborn Motor Car Company was established in 1909. The company holds the distinction of being the first to produce an automobile in Dearborn. The company failed, and the buildings were gone by 1946. *Dearborn Historical Museum.*

The saddler's shop, in the context of the arsenal, was used for making and repairing equipment for horses. It was purchased in 1877 by Dearborn Township and converted into a town hall. Township meetings were held there until 1928, when the property was sold to S.S. Kresge and the building was razed.

The gun carriage shed had a second story added on in 1906 and was used as the first headquarters of the Masonic Temple. Various businesses have occupied the building throughout the years, and there is a movement afoot to make sure that the building is preserved. It is presently the home of Cannoli Pastry. The powder magazine, which was built in 1839, was located a distance of over nine hundred feet east of the other buildings because of safety concerns. It was the last structure completed. One of the advantages of the location chosen was that it was forty feet above the branch of the Rouge River, which meant it would always be dry. Other areas on the arsenal property were low and marshy. Fourteen grated ventilators were installed to help keep the powder dry. The building's walls were built over two feet thick as a precaution should anything ignite the stored powder. It was not until August 1842 that the powder was moved from the old arsenal in Detroit to the new location. The powder was transported by rail, with horses pulling

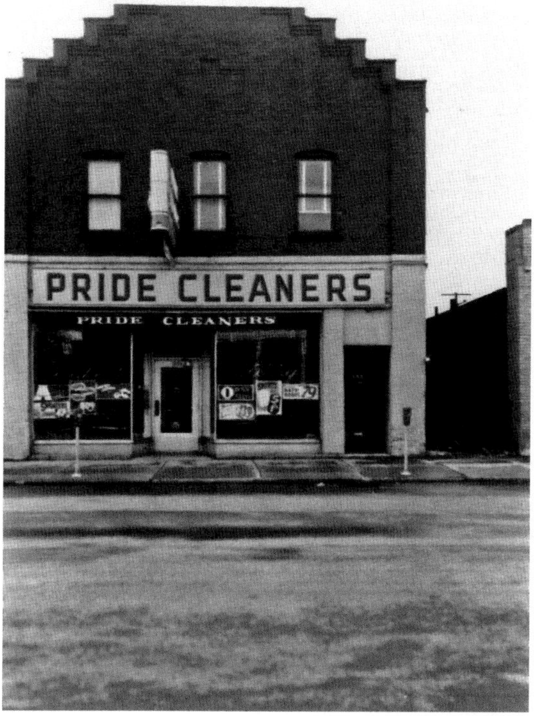

Left: The gun carriage shed had a second story added on in 1906. Various businesses have occupied the building throughout the years, including Pride Cleaners in the 1950s. The building is still standing, presently as the home of Cannoli Pastry. *Dearborn Historical Museum*.

Below: The saddler's shop, in the context of the arsenal, was used for making and repairing equipment for horses. After the arsenal closed, Dearborn Township purchased the building and converted it into a township hall. *Dearborn Historical Museum*.

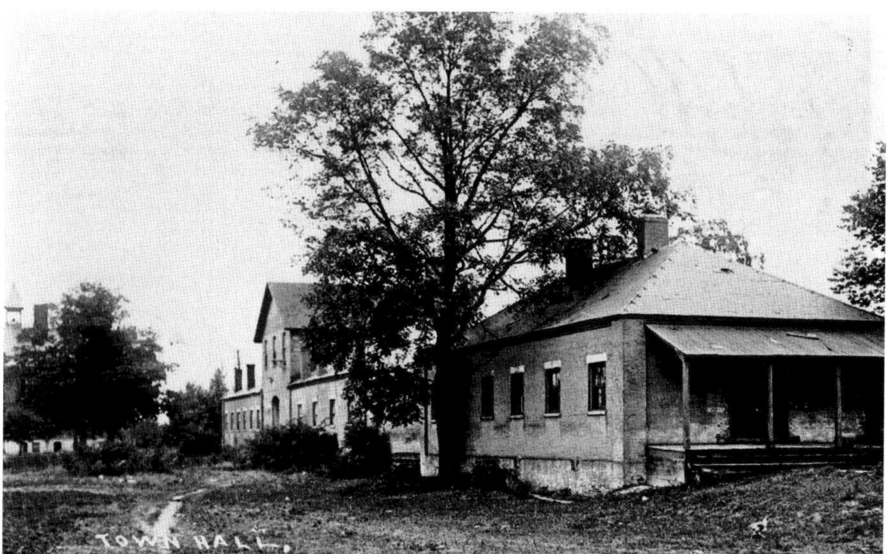

the cars. After the government closed the arsenal, it was converted into a private farm residence in 1883 by the Nathaniel Ross family. The last family member living in the house, Mary Elizabeth "Lizzie" Ross, died in 1950, and she stipulated in her will that the home and land should be given to the City of Dearborn to be used as a museum. And today, visitors can walk the halls and learn how Dearborn has changed through the years.

2
WHAT WOULD HENRY FORD THINK?

There are not many towns or cities who can claim as one of their own someone as world-renowned and as powerful a societal force as Henry Ford. If there is one word that adequately describes Ford's life, to say that he was a *complex* individual would certainly fit. But there can be no doubt that he made an indelible mark on society and certainly the area he grew up in as well. Ford grew up on a farm in what is today known as the city of Dearborn. And although he fought with his inner self as to what direction his life would take, he always found himself back in the area of his roots. And ultimately, that meant creating a very different landscape than the one in which he grew up. The story of Ford begins on a farm and ends with him being known as one of the world's foremost industrialists. And while most of the structures Ford built or that are associated with his company are still standing, there have been casualties. Some have been torn down, others have met with tragedy and still others are being used in a very different capacity than what was originally intended.

Numerous books and articles have been written about how Henry Ford came to be one of the ten most famous names in the world. In many ways, it is nothing short of miraculous that a farm boy who grew up nine miles from Detroit would grow up to transform the world and with it the land where he used to thresh hay. Ford lived the typical farm life for a boy growing up in Michigan in the nineteenth century. However, he quickly discovered that a life on the farm held little charm for him, at least, in terms of a vocation. From listening to his father's stories of the amazing new technology on display at the Centennial Exposition and tinkering with a watch he was given, the seeds of a very different life took hold. At the age of sixteen, Ford left home and walked down into Detroit to see what might catch his eye there. His intense interest in mechanical things compelled him to soak in as much as he could in machine shops. The skills Ford picked up garnered him employment with Westinghouse Road Engines, where he repaired steam engines. And just as he rose to chief engineer at the Detroit Edison Illuminating Company, his ultimate dream of an internal combustion engine loomed before him.

After crafting a successful engine and building his first vehicle, the Quadricycle, Ford had a dream to create horseless carriages for the masses. He saw automobiles as much more than just a luxury item—indeed, he saw them as powerful tools that could impact society in an amazing way. That dream led to his introduction of the now famous Model T. Add to the equation the moving assembly line and production techniques that allowed the price of a vehicle to come within range of the general public, and it would not be long before the name *Ford* was known by the masses. With all of this tremendous success came the building of numerous structures with the Ford name on them and many others that he had a hand in building, working in or living in. The development that Ford is probably most well known for consists of a two-thousand-acre area along the Rouge River. The River Rouge Plant, or Ford Rouge Plant as it became known, became the world's largest industrial complex in the world. The design of the complex was the fulfillment of the ultimate in terms of mass production. Raw materials would enter the complex, and within a matter of hours, they would be transformed into a finished product. At its peak employment in 1929, the Rouge complex employed over 103,000 workers.

When the seeds of his success had been well sown, it was Dearborn that Henry Ford chose as the place where he and his wife would build Fair Lane, an estate on the Rouge River that would serve as a home, laboratory and a place to enjoy nature. The Fords lived in the Boston Edison District of Detroit during the period that saw the Ford Motor Company have unparalleled success. It soon became apparent that Henry, Clara and their son, Edsel, were not going to be able to live any kind of peaceful life there, as a stream of uninvited guests began to encroach on their family. So, they decided to build a new home in a location where they could enjoy their privacy as well as enjoy their personal interests such as gardening and bird-watching. Ironically, the location they chose was approximately two miles from the farm where Henry was born and grew up. Over five hundred masons, woodcarvers and artisans worked on the residence, which was constructed of rough-hewn Ohio limestone. Inventor Thomas Alva Edison, who was a frequent guest at the estate, laid the cornerstone for the powerhouse. Completed in 1916, the structure was dubbed Fair Lane after the area where Ford's maternal grandfather was born in County Cork, Ireland. A separate structure was built that served as a powerhouse, making the estate self-sufficient. There were fifty-six rooms in the mansion, and the interior included such amenities as a heated pool, a bowling alley and a library, where Henry liked to sit and have Clara read to him. The estate and powerhouse are unique structures that speak to a family and a man who, in the end, made Dearborn world-famous. After Henry and Clara passed away, the complex was used by the Ford Motor Company for archival purposes, and in 1957, it was donated—along with the surrounding land—for the building of a Dearborn campus of the University of Michigan. More than one hundred years after it was completed, Fair Lane is presently being brought back to its former glory in the hopes that it will become a place of discovery, exploration and inspiration for future generations.

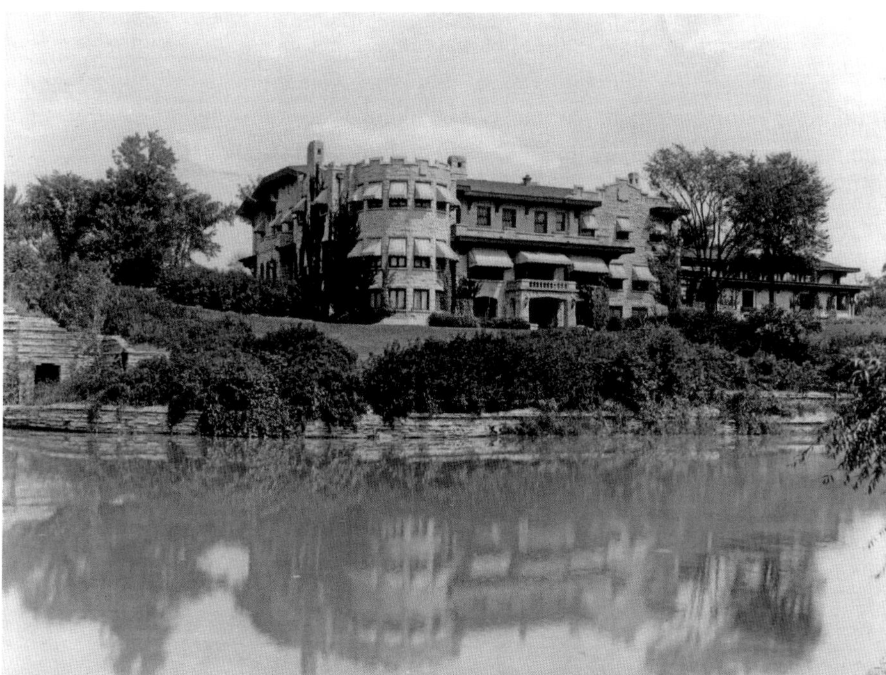

The success of the Ford Motor Company brought a stream of uninvited guests to the Fords' Detroit home. This structure, dubbed Fair Lane, was completed in 1916 and gave Henry and Clara privacy and the chance to pursue some of their interests. *Dearborn Historical Museum.*

As the success of Ford Motor Company grew to even greater heights due to the production of the Rouge Plant, Ford decided to build a headquarters near the production facility. The administration building was erected in 1927 on Schaefer Road overlooking the Rouge complex. Designed by Albert Kahn, the foremost American industrial architect of his day, the building served as the main office building for Ford and Lincoln & Mercury until 1956, when a new world headquarters was built. Edsel and Henry Ford had offices in this building, as did Harry Bennett and numerous other Ford executives. Kahn said the building was designed to "stand for 1,000 years," but unfortunately, that did not happen. The administration building was demolished in 1997.

Henry Ford continued to build. His story includes an unceasing desire for one form of construction or another. Through the years, he was the driving force behind the building of homes for Ford workers, the world's first airport hotel, an open-air museum complex known as the Edison Institute, and the list goes on. Because of Henry Ford, the Dearborn area was transformed in a very short period from a quiet countryside and farming community to a city on the world map. With the success of the Fordson Tractor, workers who flooded to the Henry Ford & Son Tractor Plant faced the fact that there was a shortage of housing. Henry Ford's solution was to establish the Dearborn Realty and Construction Company in 1919. Following his automobile production idea, there were six models one could pick from. The Ford homes were built with production-line techniques, with a specific crew performing and completing one task and then another crew coming in to perform the next task. Models were assigned lots so that the same models would never be right next to one another. Also, the homes were not placed at an equal distance from the street but were instead staggered. There were 156 homes constructed in this way, and today, they still stand happily occupied in what is known as the Ford Homes Historic District.

Another first in Henry Ford's long list of building accomplishments was the construction of the world's first airport hotel. The Dearborn Inn was built in 1931 and accommodated overnight travelers who arrived at the Ford Airport, just across Oakwood Boulevard. At the airport, built in 1924, world and national aviation history was made. Firsts were accomplished in numerous arenas, including the acceptance of all-metal airliners, radio control devices, air mail, scheduled flights and airline services. Ford was a pioneer in promoting safe, affordable air travel. He sought to achieve in aviation some of the goals that he had accomplished with automobiles. The Stout Metal Airplane Company was located on the grounds of the airport,

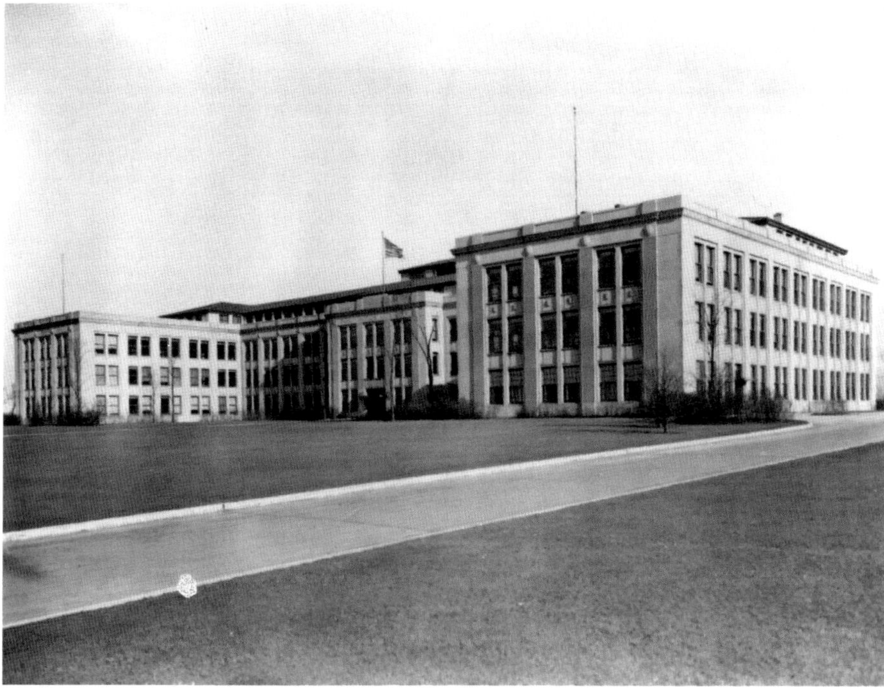

The Ford Motor Company Administration Building was built in 1927. Seen here in 1928, the building was designed by Albert Kahn and served as the main office building until 1956, when the Glass House was built. *Dearborn Historical Museum.*

and it was designated as a division of Ford Motor Company. The very first successful metal planes were built here, including the Ford Tri-Motor, which was used in the arsenals of many of the early major airlines. Charles Lindbergh was often invited to stay with the Fords at their Fair Lane estate, and he would fly into the airport. It was Lindbergh who, on one particular visit, would provide for Ford his very first plane ride. For the design of the hotel, Ford once again turned to Albert Kahn, who designed the 179-room inn in Georgian architecture style. The building features a grand ballroom and high ceilings, and its rooms are still furnished with reproductions of eighteenth- and nineteenth-century furniture. In 1937, the Dearborn Inn's accommodations were expanded with replicas of historically famous homes. Constructed near the main complex, the additions included the Barbara Fritchie House, the Patrick Henry House, the Oliver Wolcott House, the Edgar Allan Poe House and the Walt Whitman House. The airport may have closed in 1933, but the Dearborn Inn is still going strong today and provides unique accommodations and dining opportunities.

Over time, Ford became increasingly interested in preserving an American past that he more than anyone had changed. To this end, he began to collect Americana and eventually created a unique indoor/outdoor museum known as the Edison Institute. In 1919, he restored the building where he was born. In short order, he had filled an entire wing of his engineering building with artifacts. Then, on October 21, 1929, the Edison Institute was dedicated to Ford's mentor and friend, Thomas Edison, on the fiftieth anniversary of the invention of the practical incandescent lamp. The complex operated as a school where students could learn by Ford's philosophy of "learning by doing." The 240-acre complex has grown over the years to contain over one hundred historic structures, some of them original and others reproductions. By entering the many buildings, viewing the way things were and listening to the significance of changes brought on through over three hundred years of history, the story is told of a rural America and of an Industrial Revolution and innovation that swept across the country and changed life and society forever. The museum portion was built to reflect Independence Hall in Philadelphia, and it houses various artifacts that help tell the story of transportation, farming, industrialization and life in America's past. In Henry Ford's own words, when speaking of what his intentions were in building the Edison Institute, he claimed that "when we are through, we shall have reproduced American life as lived, and that, I think, is the best way of preserving at least a part of our history and tradition." Today, the complex is known as The Henry Ford, and additional attractions have been added, including the Ford Rouge Factory Tour and the Giant Screen Experience. Henry Ford's vision of bringing American history to life is being realized every day at this world-famous destination.

One of the most memorable structures that Henry Ford was associated with was designed and built for the 1933–34 Chicago World's Fair. The Ford Rotunda was built as the centerpiece of Ford's exhibit at the fair and was located on an eleven-acre plot on Lake Michigan. The Ford Drama of Transportation exhibit was housed in the central structure and was made up of sixty-seven vehicles that ranged from an Egyptian chariot to modern cars. When the fair closed in 1934, over twelve million visitors had passed through the exhibit. In 1935–36, Ford had the central building moved to Dearborn and placed across from the Ford Motor Company's Administration building on Schaefer Road. Over 650 tons of structural steel were shipped to Dearborn. It became the largest permanent industrial exhibit building in the country and was used as a reception area and orientation point for thousands of people who took tours of the famous River Rouge Plant. One of the most unique buildings to ever grace the Dearborn area, the Ford Rotunda rose twelve stories in a gear-shaped formation and was staffed by eight hundred Ford employees. The mission of the building and its many exhibits, according to Henry Ford himself, was to teach the public how things were done at Ford Motor Company.

Opened to the public on May 16, 1936, the Ford Rotunda became many things to many people. It housed a display area for new cars, an exhibit hall and a 388-seat theater. Animated exhibits demonstrated how raw materials made it to the Rouge Plant and then how the materials were transformed into a finished product. Right next to the building was a Roads of the World exhibit with a reproduction of nineteen historic roads of the world all linked together. Visitors flocked to the attraction. In the first year alone, over 900,000 visitors made their way through the doors. In the center of the building there was a huge revolving globe where

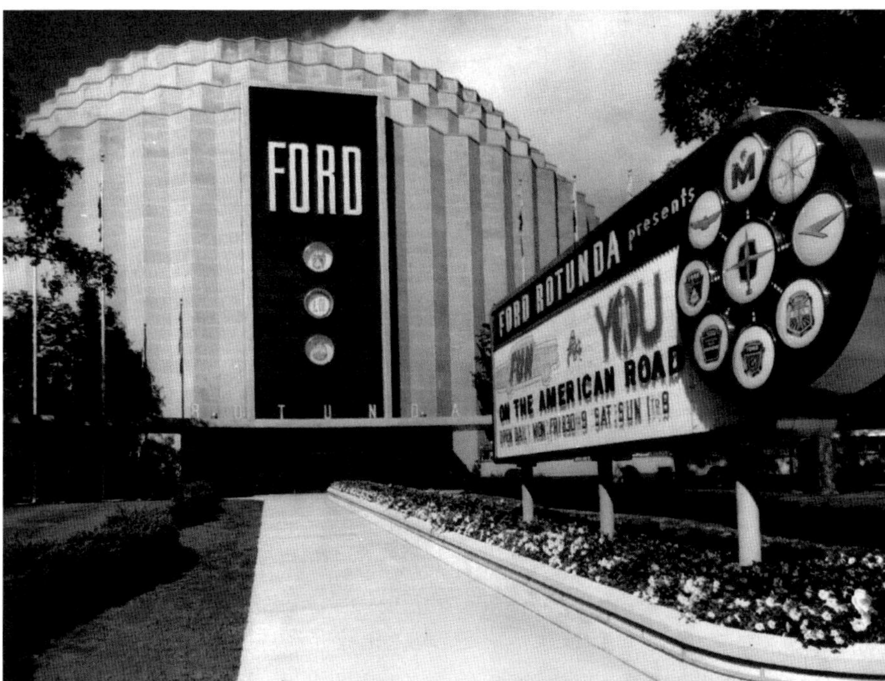

Designed and built for the 1933–34 Chicago World's Fair, Henry Ford had the main structure brought to Dearborn. It was the largest permanent industrial exhibit building in the country and became one of the most popular attractions in the world. *Dearborn Historical Museum.*

various Ford interests around the world were highlighted. In the courtyard stood a gigantic photo mural that explained manufacturing and assembly processes that went on at the Rouge Plant. Many readers will remember the tremendous Christmas displays and holiday programs. Every year from 1953 until 1961, a Christmas Fantasy area was set up. Exhibits included how Christmases past were celebrated, an enormous doll collection, local choirs singing carols and Santa Claus. For those who were so inclined, there was an opportunity to sit on Santa's lap. Sadly, tragedy struck on November 9, 1962. A fire started on the rooftop while it was being tarred. The flames spread so fast, there was no way to save the building. The intense heat weakened the steel girders, which caused slabs of limestone to split apart. The structure was destroyed in only forty minutes.

Henry Ford admired his friend and colleague Dr. George Washington Carver. Wanting to do something very special for the man who had dedicated his life to experimenting with agricultural products and to improving the yields farmers could extract from their crops, Ford had a Ford Motor Company nutrition laboratory named after Dr. Carver. Carver was present at the dedication. Located on the south side of Michigan Avenue just west of the Rouge River, the building today is being used by Beaumont Health Systems.

On the grounds of the Henry Ford Estate sat a log cabin that predated Henry Ford's ownership of the property. It was built in the mid-1800s by the Prehn family. When the Prehn family moved, Henry Ford used the cabin as a maple sugar house. The cabin made the perfect backdrop for a special program Ford would put on for family and area children at Christmastime. The children were brought to the site via horse-drawn sleigh. Santa would appear and allow the children their choice from a cabin full of new toys. Afterward, each child was given a hot bowl of Clara Ford's homemade "snowflake soup," more commonly known as oyster stew. This treat would warm them for the ride back home. After Henry Ford's death in 1947, the program continued until the passing of Clara Ford in 1950. The structure was torn down sometime during the 1950s.

As Ford Motor Company moved into a different era, a larger and different kind of structure was called for to be the headquarters of Ford Motor Company, and in 1955, construction began on Michigan Avenue not far from Southfield Freeway. The new world headquarters came to be known as the "glass house" locally because the entire building is glass faced. The building is twelve stories high and designed to accommodate three thousand employees. In addition to the prominent twelve-story office building, the

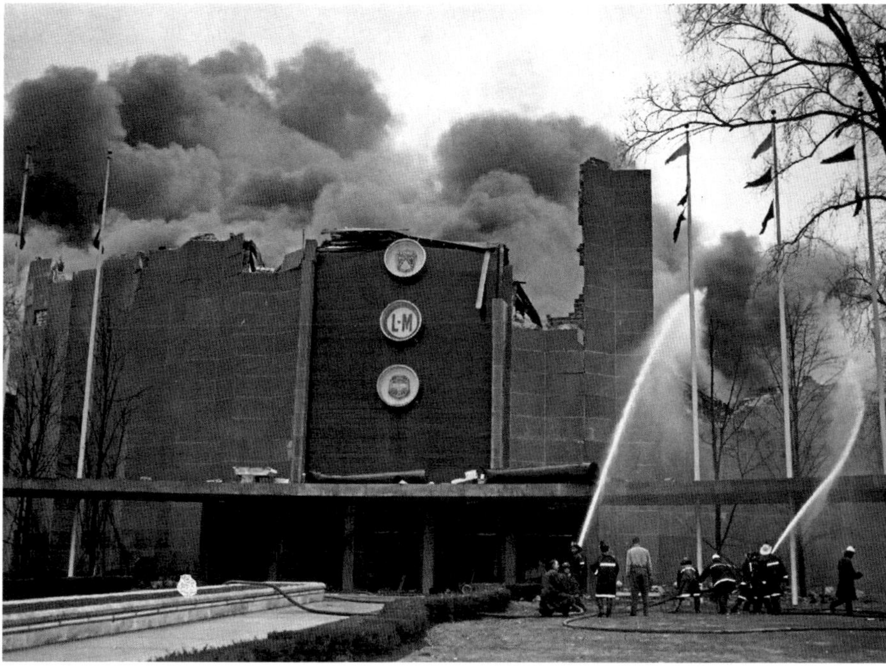

On November 9, 1962, a fire started on the Ford Rotunda's roof when a tar kettle turned over. The fire spread so fast, there was no way for the building to be saved. *Dearborn Historical Museum.*

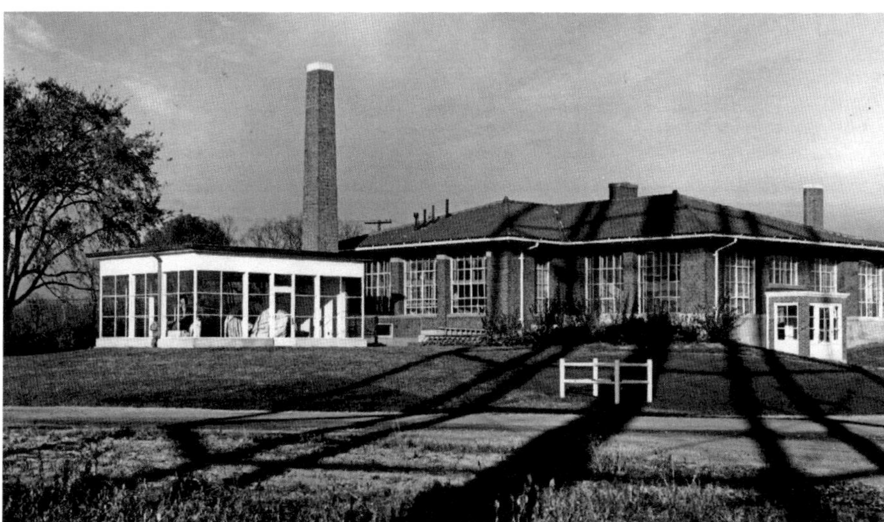

In 1942, Henry Ford set Dr. George Washington Carver up in a laboratory in an old water works building on Michigan Avenue. Experimenting with different crops, including sweet potatoes and dandelions, Carver and Ford devised a way to make a rubber substitute from goldenrod, a weed. *Dearborn Historical Museum.*

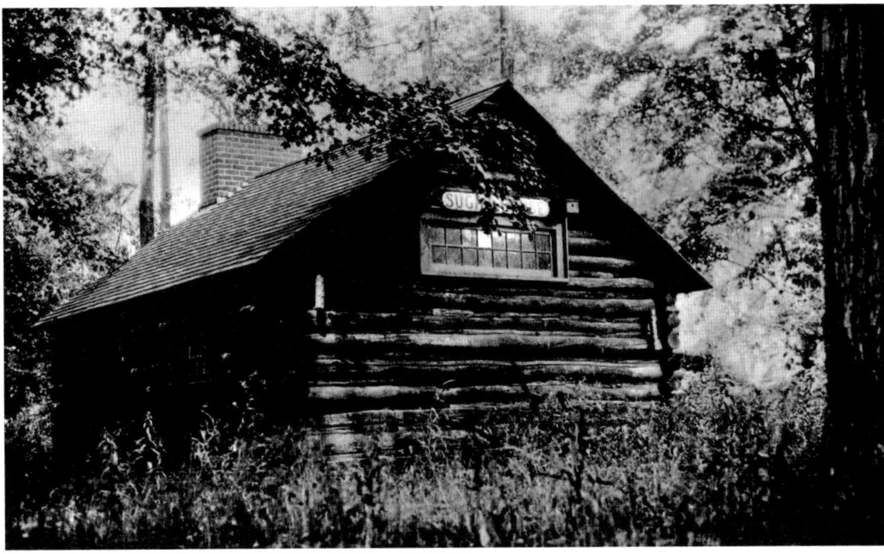

This cabin, located in the woods of Fair Lane, was used for Santa's Workshop. Area children would be given a sleigh ride to the cabin, where Santa would toss down candy from the roof and invite everyone into the cabin for hot soup and presents. *Dearborn Historical Museum.*

complex includes an adjacent three-story structure accommodating an employee cafeteria, dining rooms and a parking garage for 1,500 cars. The two elements are connected by a four-hundred-foot concourse. Some have described it as a "tall city in a park"; the complex was designed with multiple entry points to adequately service a large concentrated influx of cars on a daily basis. Located on 174 acres, most of which previously belonged to Henry Ford's private estate, the grounds are also the site of the Arjay Miller Arboretum, which features trees and shrubs native to Michigan.

While much can be said about Henry Ford and his influence, there can be no doubt that he put the City of Dearborn on the world map. And much of what he built survives to this day. And while many would love to visit the Ford Rotunda again, it is ironic that within the confines of the same city, the past has been preserved in the same area where the world was turned upside down.

3

THE SCHOOL BELL SILENCED

Dearborn has been known for many things throughout its history, and quality education is certainly one of them. Education has been a major priority from the times of the one-room schoolhouse. These early hubs of society were used to teach language, writing, reading, grammar, arithmetic, geography, history and civil government as well as morality. The textbook of the pioneer days was the McGuffey Reader, which included a wide range of educational material in addition to principles regarding ethical behavior. And although textbooks and methods changed through the years, what did not change was the quality of education and the fondness that folks from Dearborn still have for their school years. Over the years, there have been periods of tremendous growth as well as diminishing attendance, which have caused everything from a surge in the construction of schools to numerous decommissioned buildings. The images and information in this chapter are meant to serve as a dedication to these very special institutions. Many area residents will well remember the sound of the school bell in telling the story of an area known for high-quality school facilities as well as a great education. And throughout the years, Dearbornites have grown to see their school system as a tremendous source of pride. Many of the structures have either been lost to history or now serve in another capacity but they still live on in the hearts and minds of former students.

One of the first schools in the area was the Scotch Settlement School, which was so named because it was a place where mostly Scots-Irish settlers had established farms. Built in 1838 and located on a corner of the

Richard Gardner farm, this was a one-story frame structure with benches and desks along the outside walls of the room. The building was destroyed by fire, and a new brick school was built near what is today Warren Avenue and Southfield Road in 1861. It was this schoolhouse that Henry Ford walked into in 1871 at the age of seven. Ford had it moved in 1929 to become part of his outdoor museum and the Greenfield Village School System. It now stands to teach adults and children alike about how a one-room schoolhouse operated.

Another early school, the Miller School, was built near Michigan Avenue and Miller Road in 1830. In fact, three different buildings have occupied roughly the same piece of land. The first structure was a log cabin school. In 1856, this structure was replaced with a frame building, which Henry Ford and Eleanor Woodworth attended in the 1870s. By 1918, the frame school had deteriorated; it was torn down, and the present building was erected. A replica of the frame version was built in 1943 by Henry Ford and stands in Greenfield Village. The present Miller School is the second-oldest school building in Dearborn. The original construction called for eight

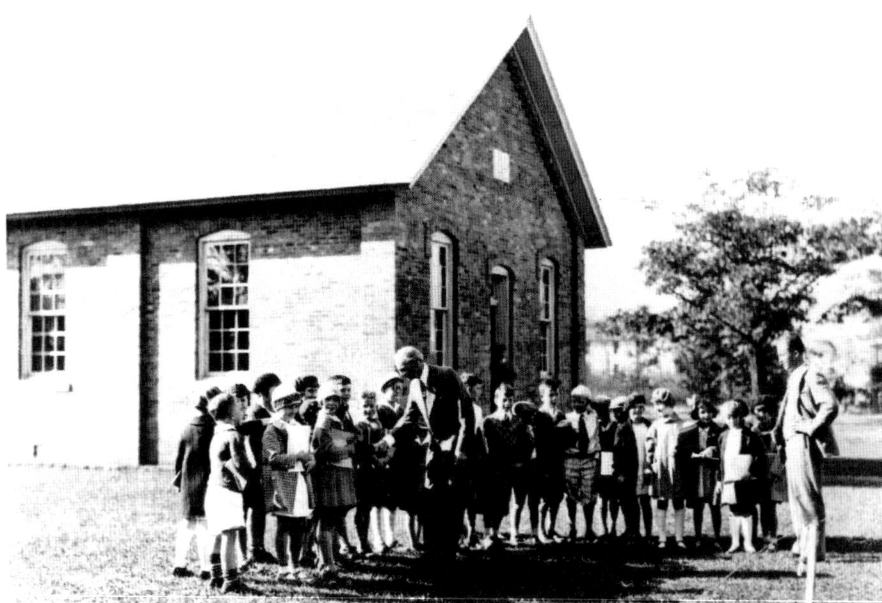

The Scotch Settlement School, built in 1861 and originally located on the north side of Warren between Southfield and Greenfield, was the first school that Henry Ford attended. Ford had the building moved to Greenfield Village in 1929. *Dearborn Historical Museum.*

rooms. The building has gone through numerous additions and structural changes through the years. When the Rouge Plant began to add hundreds of new workers, the need to expand the building brought major additions. By the fall of 1921, high school classes had been added, and the school provided classes for kindergarten through twelfth grade. Not only were new classrooms added but also a gymnasium, an auditorium, a cafeteria, a music room, an art room, a library, a homemaking room, new offices, a health room, a new kindergarten section and a large shop room. When Fordson High School officially opened in 1927, seventh through twelfth grades moved there. Elementary enrollment reached an all-time high at Miller School in 1927 with 11,125 students and forty-five teachers for kindergarten through sixth grade. During World War II, the building was used by the Red Cross and the Rationing Board. In 1949, the basement and two-thirds of the classroom space were used by the newly formed Dearborn Junior College. For the next fourteen years, Miller School was used for elementary-age and junior college programming. When Henry Ford Community College opened in 1963, the building then became home to the administrative staff of the Dearborn Public Schools until the Ten Eyck Center was adapted for that purpose beginning in 1977. To the present, Miller School version number three continues on as an elementary school.

In 1906, Peter Roulo donated land in Springwells Township on the border of Detroit to be used for a new school building. The first structure to be built on the site was named after Roulo and was a wooden two-room building. When the Springwells Township School system was established in 1920, the Roulo building became a part of it and serviced kindergarten through fifth grade. After only one year, the structure was used for only kindergarten and first grade, and the rest of the grades were transferred over to Salina. But things changed when, by 1925, there was a desperate need for additional space. The City of Springwells purchased land adjacent to the school and began construction on a twelve-room, one-story school. The building was dedicated in 1926, and due to structural problems at Salina, the new school was immediately overcrowded. On a temporary basis, Roulo students had classes in the morning, Salina students had classes in the afternoon and high school students were taught wherever space could be found. This situation was corrected when Salina was completed in 1927. From 1930 until 1960, Roulo School operated as an elementary facility. But by 1960, with Salina able to handle the educational needs of the area, the Dearborn Board of Education had decided to close Roulo. For a few years, the building was leased to the Ambassador Baptist Church.

By 1965, there was much discussion about how the building should be used, and this debate went on for years. However, in 1972, a fire that was ruled vandalism prompted the vacating of the building, and it remained empty until it was torn down in 1979.

With the growth of Ford Motor Company in the 1920s, new neighborhoods began to spring up, and there was a tremendous need for additional schools. A good example of this is the Thayer School, which was built in 1924 to replace a one-room schoolhouse and provide room for the potential growth. The school was named in honor of the entire Thayer family. Nahum P. Thayer arrived in Greenfield Township in 1820 at the age of eighteen. He soon cleared land for a farm and house and established a farm that was owned by his descendants for many years. Thayer helped build the first three miles of the Chicago Road (now Michigan Avenue) out of Detroit. He held various local offices and served as a colonel in the state militia. In 1842, he leased land to Richard McDonald for the purposes of establishing a school and church building on the land. The one-room schoolhouse was known as the McDonald School and was located near Warren and Wyoming. Years later, when the new structure replaced the McDonald School, it seemed fitting that the new one be named after the Thayer family. At the time of its construction, the new school was considered the most modern building of its kind—so much so that representatives of other districts would visit the school to study it. After just two years, the school was overcrowded to the point where the locker rooms and storerooms were being used as classrooms. In 1927, with the opening of Oakman School and Lowrey Junior High, the problem was alleviated. However, as the Rouge Plant continued its explosive growth, there was such an influx of students to Thayer that many had to be bused to Miller School. The school remained stable until the late 1950s, when enrollment declined to the point that the school was closed. It was decided that it would be best to sell the building to the Pius Society of St. Paul for $51,000. And it remains in that organization's hands to the present.

Schools like Coonville were a very important part of this growing area. Located near Ann Arbor Trail and Outer Drive, the school was named for the small settlement founded by the Valentine Coon family. After the original school building burned down, the school pictured in this book was completed in 1899 by then Dearborn Township school board member Paul Gillow. In 1947, the structure was coated with bricks. It was then torn down in 1950 when the Clara B. Ford Elementary School expanded. Throughout the history of the area, there has always been a battle to keep up with explosions in population at various times. For instance, in 1915, when

Henry Ford started building tractors, there was an almost immediate need for additional school buildings and classrooms. So, in 1916, construction began at the corner of Garrison and Monroe Streets on what would become known as Garrison Elementary. In 1937, the school was renamed Salisbury after a beloved figure, Harry Salisbury, who had come to Dearborn in 1908 as a superintendent and teacher and who served over forty years in an educational capacity. The building was used as an elementary facility until 1972, when it was upgraded to be used in the adult and continuing education arena. It still stands today but is now being used by Imam Mahdi Association of Marjaeya (IMAM), whose goal is to cultivate a vibrant, collaborative and supportive Muslim community of strong faith and good citizenry.

The history of parochial schools in the Dearborn area is every bit as rich as the story of public education. From the pioneer days until more recent times, religious schools have served as a way not only to educate but also to preserve religious and ethnic heritage. The story of St. Alphonsus is an interesting study in that the school was actually founded before the church. In order to serve the growing German Catholic immigrant population, in 1846, a simple log cabin was built near what is now Warren Avenue and Schaefer. The course work consisted of German reading, English reading, arithmetic and religious instruction. When the log cabin began to deteriorate, a frame school was built in 1855 on land donated by the Esper family for the express purpose of a church, school and pastor's house. When the population outgrew the frame structure, a new brick school was constructed and used until 1921. An exciting new era began in 1922, when the first unit was completed of what would eventually be a large campus that served kindergarten through twelfth grade. The school thrived for decades until declining enrollment forced the closing of the high school in 2003, and the grade school followed shortly thereafter. The high school building was briefly occupied by a charter school but has been vacant for the last several years.

In the early 1950s, the baby boom brought hundreds of students to the doors of the elementary schools of Dearborn. Not surprisingly, this caused major overcrowding in many of the schools, particularly Long and Oxford schools. To solve this problem, plans were drawn up for a new facility. It was named the David P. Lapham School in honor of an early pioneer and foundational figure. The Lapham family had been a vital part of Dearborn for generations. They owned a one-hundred-acre farm near what is today Military and Monroe Streets. The family also operated a general store and a butcher shop. David Lapham was born in 1851, and he established

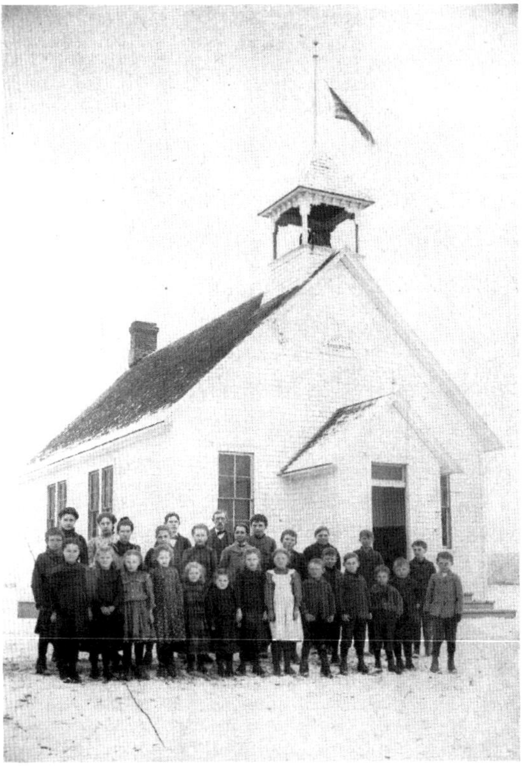

Left: The area's great public education legacy began with one-room schoolhouses like the Coonville School, here pictured in 1906. These schools were attended by a large age range, usually from five to eighteen years of age. *Dearborn Historical Museum.*

Below: Garrison Elementary was built in 1916 on the corner of Garrison and Monroe. In 1937, it was renamed Salisbury after Henry Salisbury, who dedicated his life to the education of students. *Dearborn Historical Museum.*

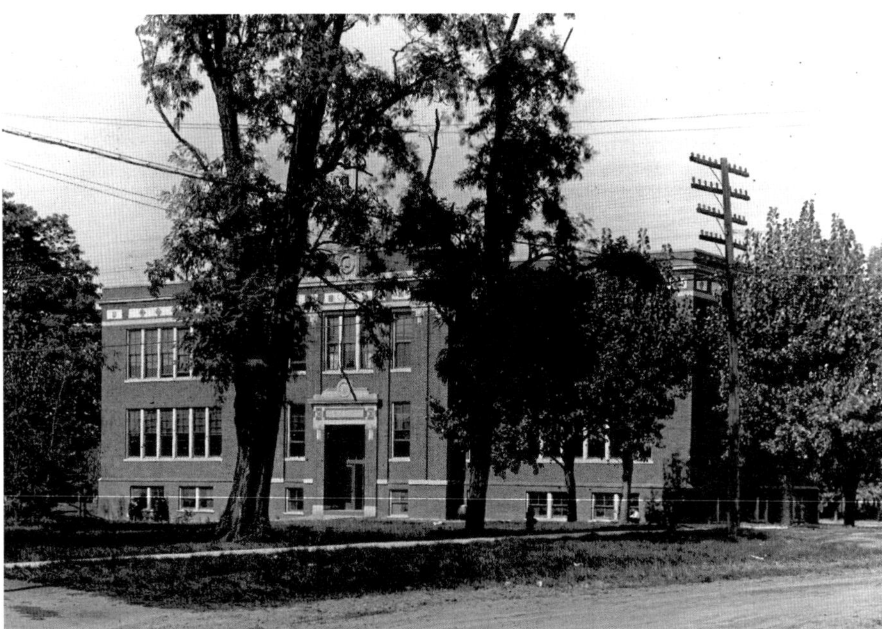

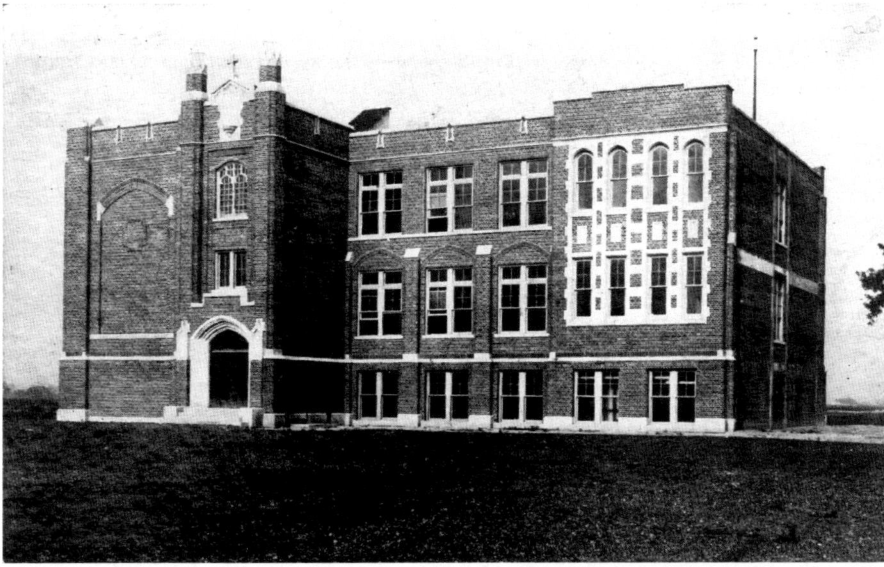

Dating back to 1846, there has been some form of St. Alphonsus School. In 1922, the first unit was completed of what would eventually be a large campus that served kindergarten through twelfth grade. *Dearborn Historical Museum.*

Dearborn's first bank in 1896, which he eventually sold to Henry Ford in 1916. Lapham also served on the board of education when Dearborn's first high school was built, and in his day, he advocated building a school to prevent overcrowding long before it was even needed. Declining enrollment caused the closing of the school in 1972, and the building has now been transformed and serves the educational needs of the West Village Academy.

However, not all of the school buildings that have been a part of this area's educational history are connected to local names; some have been named for more famous, national figures. Cases in point include Lindbergh Elementary, named after famous aviator Charles Lindbergh, and Edison School, which was dedicated on the eighty-fifth anniversary of Thomas Edison's birth. When Thomas Alva Edison came to Dearborn in 1929 for the dedication of the Edison Institute, the construction of the school building that would bear his name was already underway. The land around the Edison school was used for recreation for the surrounding community. It was a Dearborn architect, Harry Vicary, who designed the school to be a two-story brick building with ten classrooms, a kindergarten room, a library, an auditorium and a gymnasium. The school opened on January 26, 1931, and was formally dedicated on February 11, 1932. The principle

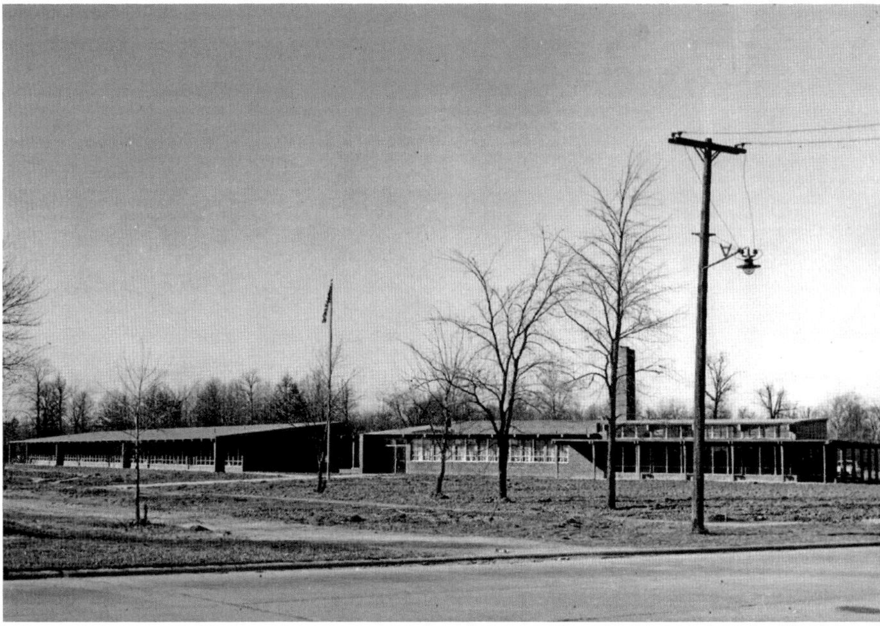

The David P. Lapham School helped alleviate overcrowding in the 1950s. After a very short lifetime, declining enrollment caused the closing of the school in 1972. *Dearborn Historical Museum.*

speaker at the dedication was William J. Cameron, a personal friend of Edison. Mrs. Edison and son Charles were invited to attend as special guests but unfortunately could not make it. The school was expanded by 1940 to include both elementary as well as junior high classes. In 1952, a major expansion took place with the building of thirty-six new classrooms, a new auditorium, a gymnasium, an expanded library, a cafeteria, three complete shops, a home economics room, an art room, an audio-visual room and band and choral rooms. A year later, a swimming pool was built. By 1978, the school had closed, and the building was razed not long afterward.

Dearbornites have long been proud of the academic tradition that has become a part of the fabric that makes this area something special. And one of the schools that will always be remembered as carrying that banner of academic excellence was located near Oxford Street and Telegraph Road. With the building and development of the Ford Motor Company's Engineering Laboratories and Tractor Plant, the neighborhood just south of Michigan Avenue between Monroe Street and Telegraph Road began to experience tremendous growth. In 1919, all of Dearborn's students in that neighborhood attended Garrison School. Southwestern School (now

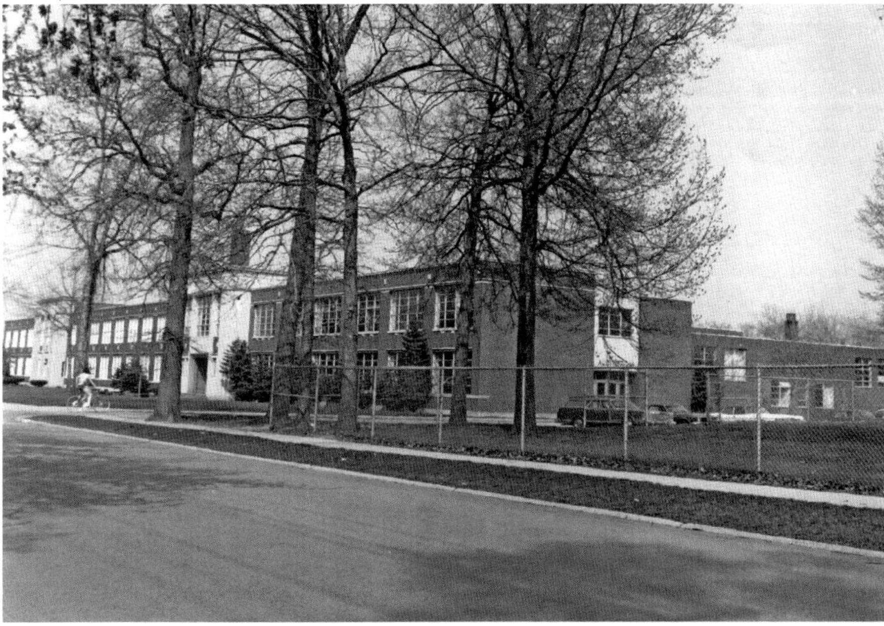

Named for famous inventor Thomas Alva Edison, this school was dedicated on the eighty-fifth anniversary of his birth in 1932. At one point, it provided classes for both elementary and junior high students. *Dearborn Historical Museum.*

Duvall) was built in 1921 to relieve overcrowding. But there was still a problem with high enrollment, and it was proposed that a new school be built near Oxford Street and Telegraph Road. Oxford School opened in 1924 and, at first, serviced both elementary and junior high students. As the neighborhood expanded, so did the enrollment. In 1935, the entire ninth grade was moved to Dearborn High School, and in 1953, all of the junior high students moved into the new O.L. Smith Junior High School. By 1951, there were 810 students attending Oxford, when the official capacity was supposed to only be 800. It was the first school in Dearborn to teach science through the use of a science center, and an annual science fair was instituted in 1941. During the 1970s, enrollment fell dramatically, and despite efforts by citizens to stop it, the school was closed and torn down in 1979.

Just after World War II, West Dearborn went through a tremendous growth period. New houses were being built at a fast clip, and one of the neighborhoods that needed a school was the subdivision between Oakwood and Outer Drive. Initially, in 1945, a five-room school was constructed, but as the surrounding neighborhood continued to grow, it became evident there would need to be a major expansion. In 1956, the school was enlarged from

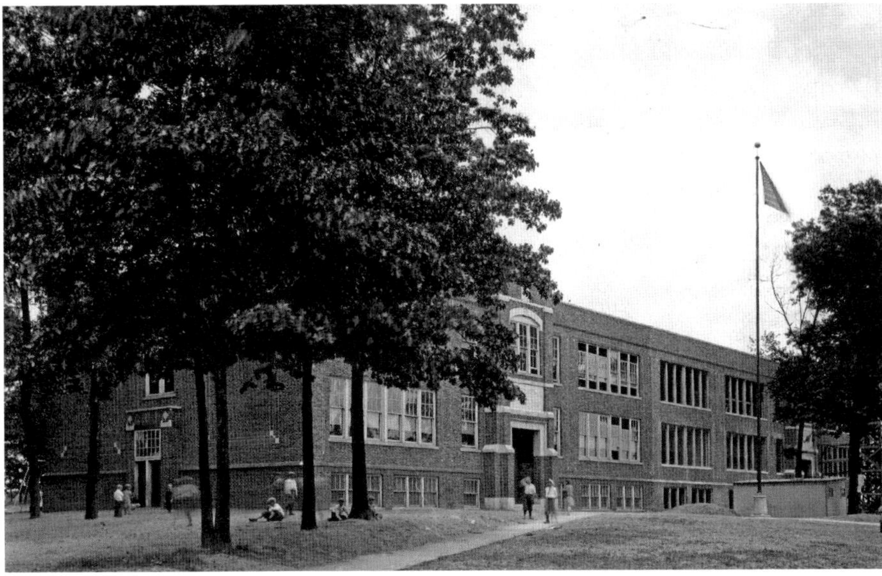

Located on Oxford Street between Cornell and Geneva, this was the first school in Dearborn to teach science through the use of a science center and an annual science fair, which was instituted in 1941. *Dearborn Historical Museum.*

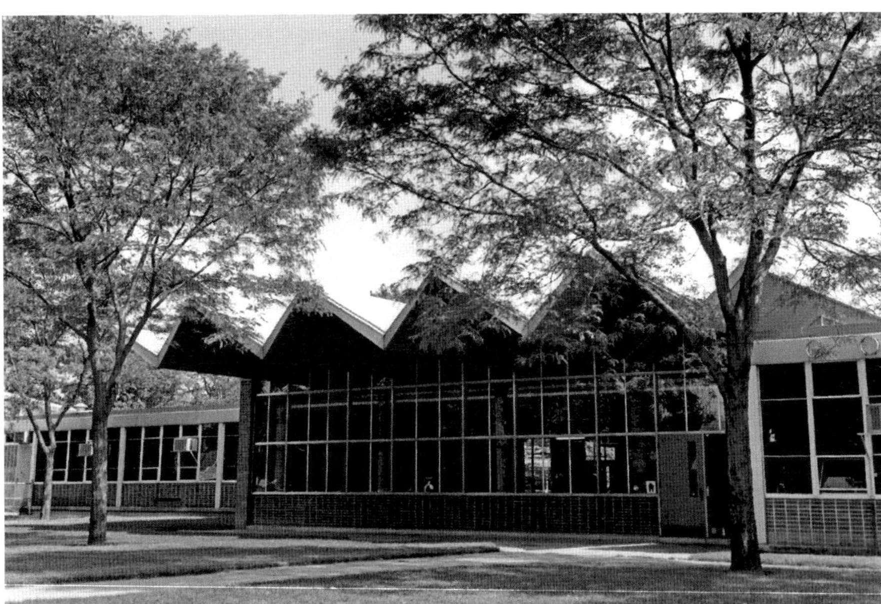

Ten Eyck School, built in 1945, was expanded in the 1950s and included a unique design, incorporating a five-sided courtyard in the center of the building that was used to plant gardens for science class. *Dearborn Historical Museum.*

six classrooms to sixteen, and enrollment soared to over five hundred. Also added was a library, a gymnasium, a science workroom, a kitchen and a multipurpose room. There were no outside corridors; instead, the school had a unique five-sided courtyard in the center of the building, used to plant gardens for science class. The school was named after one of the area's earliest settlers, Conrad Ten Eyck. He moved to Detroit from New York in 1802. Ten Eyck then moved to Dearbornville in 1823 and built the Ten Eyck Tavern in 1826 on what was then called the Chicago Road (today Michigan Avenue). The school that bore his name was closed in 1976 due to declining enrollment, and the building now serves as the administration offices of the Dearborn Public Schools and is used to teach special classes and workshops for both teachers and students.

The tremendous expansion of the school system had residents turning to early pioneer names when it came time to name a new school building. In the case of the William H. Clark School, which opened in 1951, this was certainly the case. Clark had moved to Dearborn after the Civil War, and he was a major advocate of constructing a new brick school building on the corner of Garrison Street and Monroe Street. Many Dearbornites thought that the building would never be filled, but Clark continued to promote the financing and construction of the building. The structure was built in 1893 and housed all of the district's students from first grade through high school in seven rooms. A couple of generations later, Clark's dedication was honored with a school that bore his name at Silvery Lane and Lawrence. The unusual feature of the building was that it resembled a one-story ranch. This school allowed overcrowding to be relieved at Haigh School. Due to declining enrollment, the school was closed in June 1976 and no longer stands.

One of the last schools to be built in the postwar building boom, the Louis B. Howe School on Oakwood Boulevard, opened in September 1955. It was named for one of Dearborn's pioneers, Louis Howe, the son of Elba Howe, Dearbornville's station agent for the Michigan Central Railroad and the community's first undertaker. Louis was born in 1873 and served as township clerk and treasurer. When the Village of Dearborn was incorporated, he became the village clerk and treasurer. He personally conducted the 1900 census in Dearborn, counting not just people but chickens as well. To say that Howe was a man of many hats would be an understatement, as he served on the school board, was a charter member of the Dearborn Rotary Club, served as master of the Masonic Lodge and volunteered as Dearborn's fire chief. An insurance salesman, he also followed in his father's footsteps in becoming a funeral director. Howe was a very good friend of Henry Ford, and he encouraged Ford to build the Dearborn Country Club and to help Dearborn High School, which badly needed an athletic field. The result was the use of Ford Field for school activities. The school building that bore Howe's name was designed in such a way that it featured a walk-through classroom setup instead of long corridors. The completion of the school could not have come at a better time, as it relieved overcrowding at Snow and Ten Eyck Schools at a time when the neighborhood around Oakwood Hospital was rapidly expanding. When told that a school was going to be named for him, Howe commented that having schools named after people in his family was becoming a tradition, as his wife was the daughter of William Clark, after whom Clark School had been named. The 1970s saw declining enrollment, and it was suggested that Howe should be closed, but a dramatic school board meeting saved the school for a few more years. By 1978, however, enrollment had declined to the point where the facility was forced to close. For years, the building was used by the Dearborn Public Schools as a training facility, but that function has now ceased. Today, the building is for sale.

Another structure that has gone through quite a transformation and that many Dearbornites remember fondly was erected on Mason Street and served as Dearborn High School starting in 1926. When a larger high school was built in 1957 on Outer Drive and students of Dearborn High were moved there, the building on Mason Street underwent extensive remodeling and became Ray Adams Junior High. The class of June 1957 was the last Dearborn High class to graduate from the building on Mason Street. The following September, the second and third floors were opened as a ninth-grade facility, while the seventh and eighth grades were added in the fall of 1958. It was named for the former superintendent of schools who oversaw tremendous growth in the Dearborn educational system, Ray H. Adams, who arrived in the Detroit area in 1917 seeking a teaching position. He applied to several districts, but the only one that replied was Dearborn District no. 7. The reply informed him that there would be a vacancy very soon and that the opening was for the position of superintendent of Dearborn schools. At first, he didn't think he was interested, but when he passed by Dearborn on the train, he had second thoughts. His career highlights are many, including the building of six new school buildings, the introduction of music into the schools, the establishment of domestic science and printing in the high school and the inclusion of art and the merger of the Fordson and Dearborn School

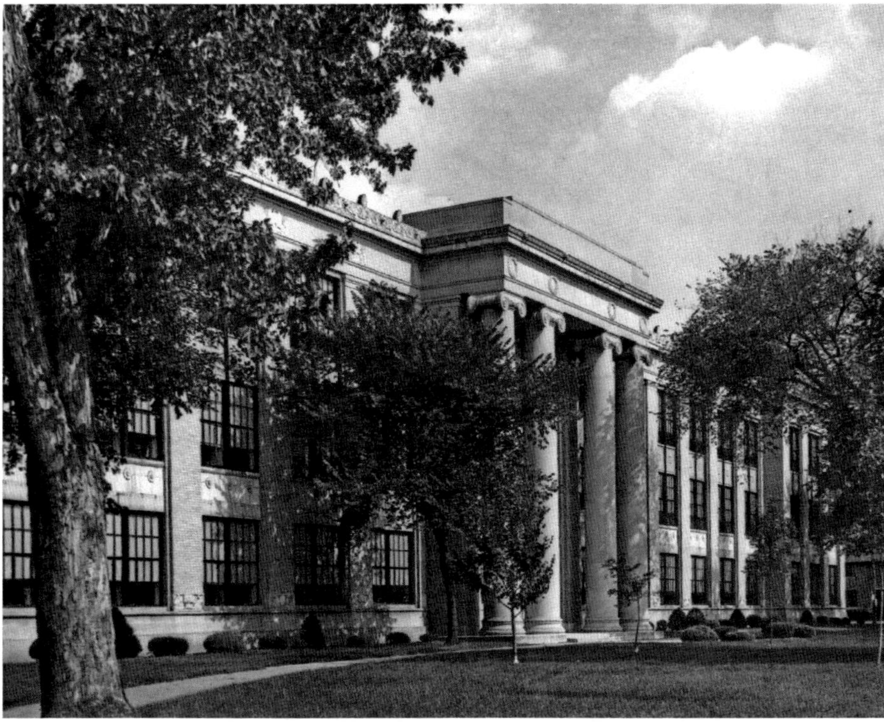

Erected in 1925, this structure served as Dearborn High School until 1957. It then became Ray H. Adams Junior High School. It served students until 1982, and the building has been transformed into an office complex. *Dearborn Historical Museum.*

Districts in 1944. Adams Junior High served students well until 1982, when the doors of 835 Mason closed after fifty-six years of service. Today, the building has been beautifully transformed and updated and it houses the Dearborn Atrium Office Center.

The proud tradition of excellent education and dedicated teachers and students continues until the present day. And while the ebb and flow of population has caused much change in terms of the building and closing of schools, that process has never taken the heart and passion out of the leaders and residents of Dearborn for providing what they know is one of the most important gifts a person can be given: a quality education.

4
LIGHTS, CAMERA, NO ACTION

After World War I, cinemas became an increasingly popular form of entertainment for the masses, and Dearborn was certainly ready to partake in this exciting new format. As the population of Dearborn expanded in the early 1900s, the need for entertainment outlets increased, and the cinema was one way this craving could be fulfilled. The first motion picture house in Dearborn was located on Monroe Street. The movies shown were from the silent era early on, and there was a pianist who played along with the action, with the idea of creating the mood necessary for each scene. Interestingly for the audience, however, this effort oftentimes woefully failed and could even be characterized as rather ridiculous because the pianist had not been shown the film beforehand. The result was the playing of inappropriate music in conjunction with a scene that called for something totally different to what people were viewing on the screen.

One structure that served in this capacity and additionally as a multipurpose building was the beautiful Calvin Theater, which was located on Michigan Avenue in West Dearborn. Opened in 1927 on the same spot where the Ten Eyck Memorial Methodist-Episcopal Church once stood, the Calvin became a tremendously popular venue and is still fondly remembered by many today. The building seated 1,485. Early on, the structure served as host to both vaudeville acts as well as films. On August 26, 1929, the Calvin featured its first talking picture when there was a showing of the Oscar award–winning *Broadway Melody*. The Calvin was used for something very special specifically related to Dearborn on November 8, 1929. A private newsreel showing of

Light's Golden Jubilee was viewed there by Henry Ford, Edsel Ford, R.W. Bowli of Paramount and H.S. Koppin, owner of the theater. These were scenes of the events of October 21, 1929, when Thomas Edison himself re-created the lighting of the first practical incandescent light during the dedication of the Edison Institute. Over the years, the Calvin was used for showing first-rate films such as *Gone with the Wind* and hosting plays and functions such as political rallies. It was a cheap form of entertainment where patrons could get a lot of enjoyment for their money, including cartoons, newsreels and feature films for just a few pennies. There was a row of small stores that inhabited the ground floor of the theater. In 1939, one of the shops that moved in was known as the Maryland Sweet Shop. Later, the location became known as the Calvin Sweet Shop, and it quickly became one of the most popular sweet shops in the area. Unfortunately, after several fires that left the interior gutted, the building was torn down in 1981.

In July 1940, construction began on a state-of-the art theater at 5746 Schaefer. The building design incorporated many features that would attract patrons. Because the building utilized classic art deco elements, it had a very

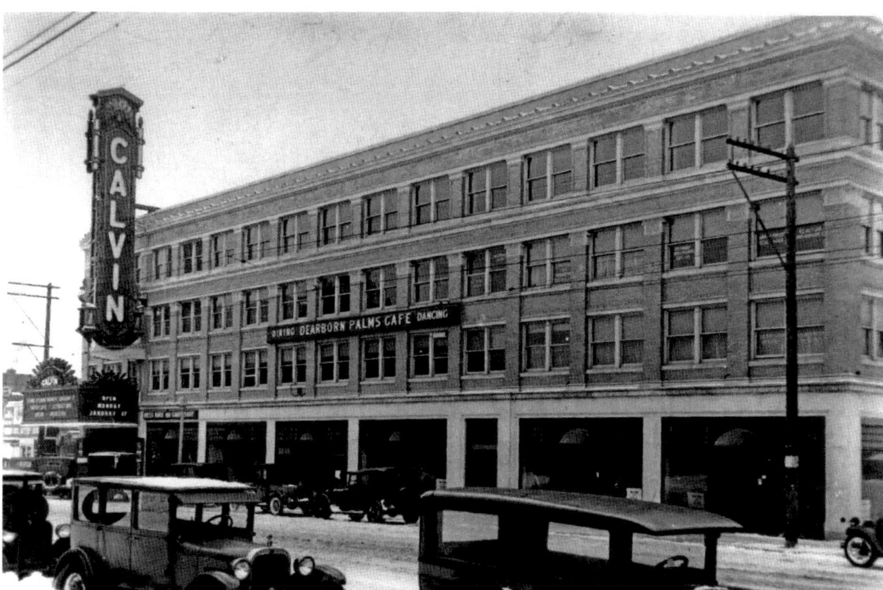

Opening night for the Calvin Theater was January 17, 1927. The beautiful facility was used for first-rate films, plays and functions, such as political rallies. *Dearborn Historical Museum.*

modern look. The main entrance was a three-story semi-attached round tower that gave the appearance of being transmission gears stacked one on top of the other. The unique marquee was reminiscent of the Ford Rotunda. The theater was named after the opera *Carmen*, and artists were hired to create colorful and thematic murals depicting the tragic love story on the interior. The seating capacity could accommodate 1,500. The Carmen operated for thirty-three years but, due to declining attendance, closed its doors in 1974. For a short time, the theater seating was stripped out and the interior was used by an auto supply store, but that operation was short-lived and the building was demolished.

Another theater located in east Dearborn was the Midway Theatre. The Midway was a small, neighborhood-type movie house located in the main business district just north of the intersection of Michigan Avenue and Schaefer Road. It opened in 1935 and was designed by the architecture firm of Bennett & Straight, well known for its designs of many of the area's entertainment venues. In fact, Bennett & Straight also designed another local area theater, the new Circle Theater (later known as the Camelot 1-2-3), on West Warren Avenue at Miller Road. The Midway featured a single screen, and the seating capacity was around six hundred. During its heyday, one of the more popular actresses to grace the Midway screen was Shirley Temple. When one of her films was released, the Midway was one of the first area theaters to receive it, and the theater would be decorated both inside and out with Shirley Temple memorabilia and film-related items. Also, what made the Midway so popular during its time of operation was the fact that one admission price would allow a patron to sit and watch whatever was playing over and over for hours. The theater closed in 1952. The building was repurposed into a retail facility, and the original auditorium was demolished, leaving the lobby portion of the building. Today, only the façade remains.

The Circle Theater mentioned above opened in 1937 at 12715 West Warren Avenue. After the grand opening, the theater was featured in the January 8, 1938 issue of *BoxOffice* magazine, which detailed the unique design attributes. The theater was built to be spacious and comfortable, with auditorium seating for 1,800 patrons. There was a large foyer, a circular rotunda approximately thirty-eight feet in diameter, a lobby that measured twenty-seven by forty-two feet, a large projection room, retiring rooms, management offices and property rooms, as well as two stores. And there was plenty of room for displays of coming attractions and current offerings. The City of Dearborn held Christmas parties for schoolchildren at theaters like

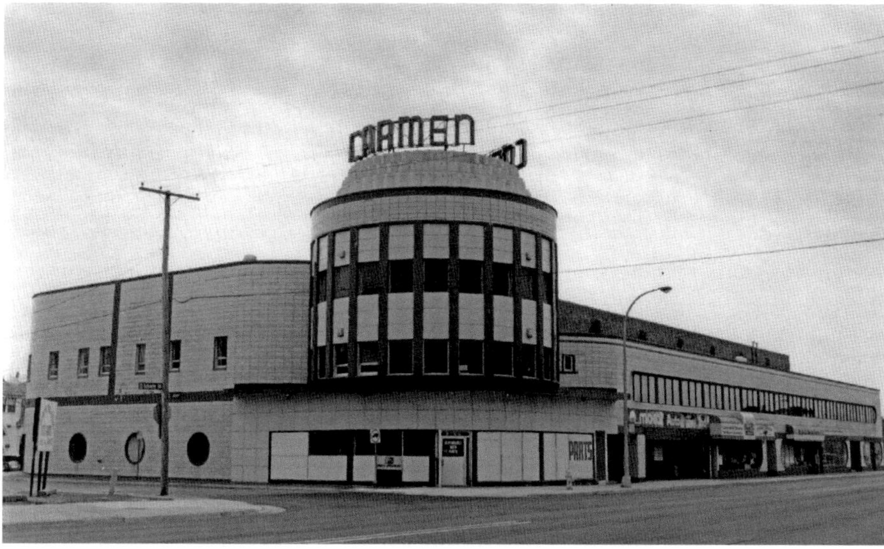

You can't miss the classic art deco elements in the Carmen Theater. The seating capacity was 1,500, and the unique marquee was reminiscent of the Ford Rotunda. *Dearborn Historical Museum.*

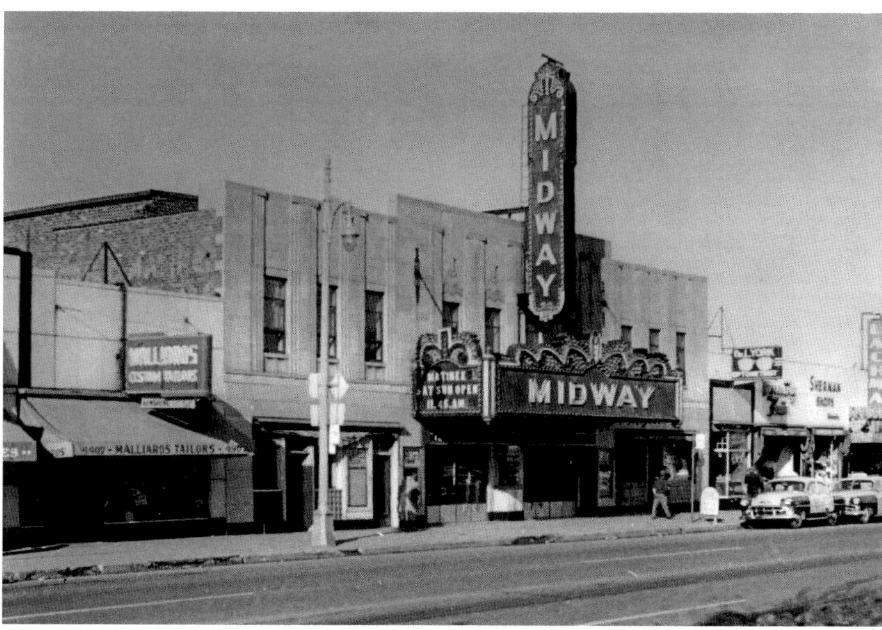

Opened in 1935, the Midway Theater was located on Schaefer Road just north of Michigan Avenue. A popular feature at the Midway was that patrons could remain and watch the same movie over and over again. *Dearborn Historical Museum.*

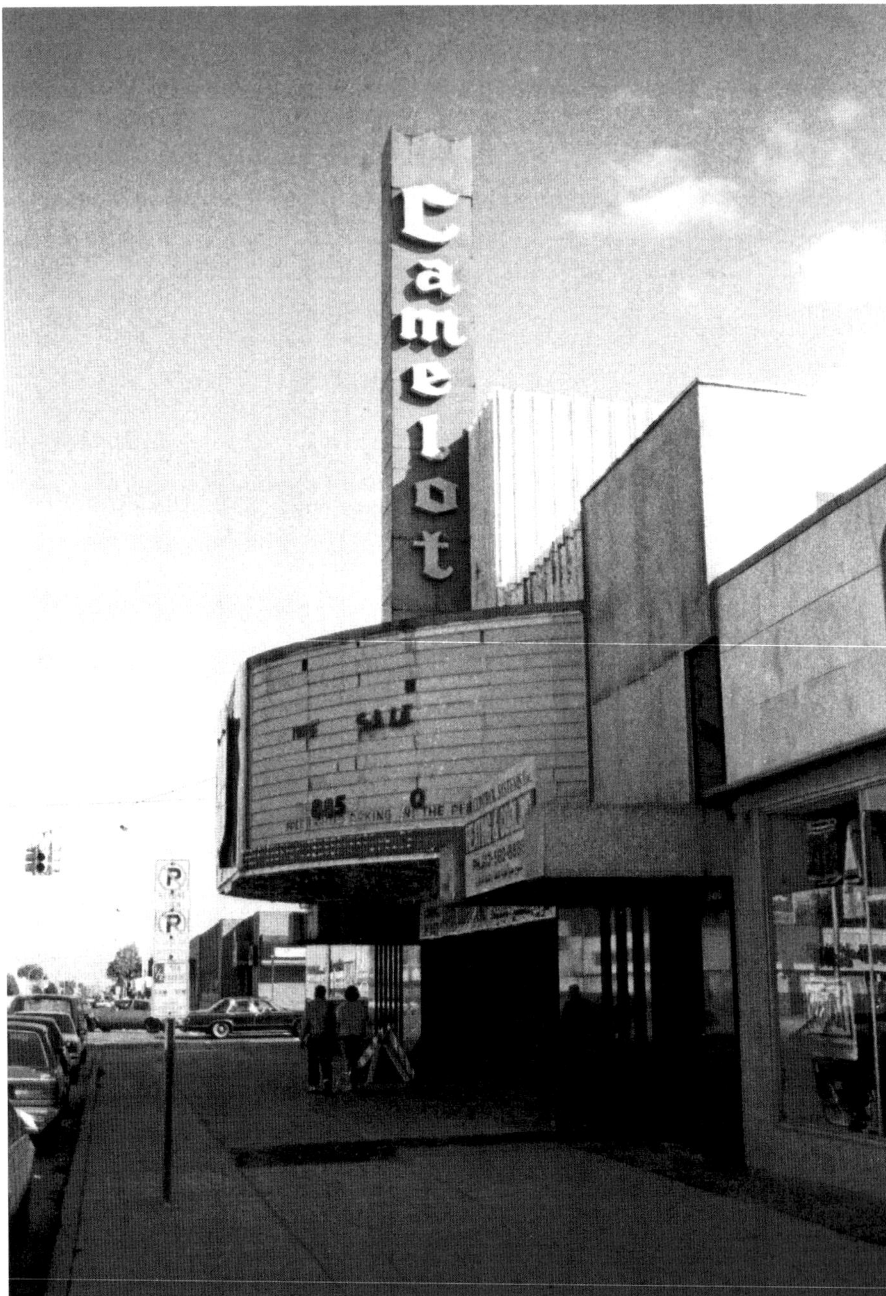

In 1937, the Circle Theater opened at 12715 West Warren Avenue. The auditorium seated 1,800, and the building had some unique design attributes. In the early 1960s, new owners renamed it the Camelot. *Dearborn Historical Museum.*

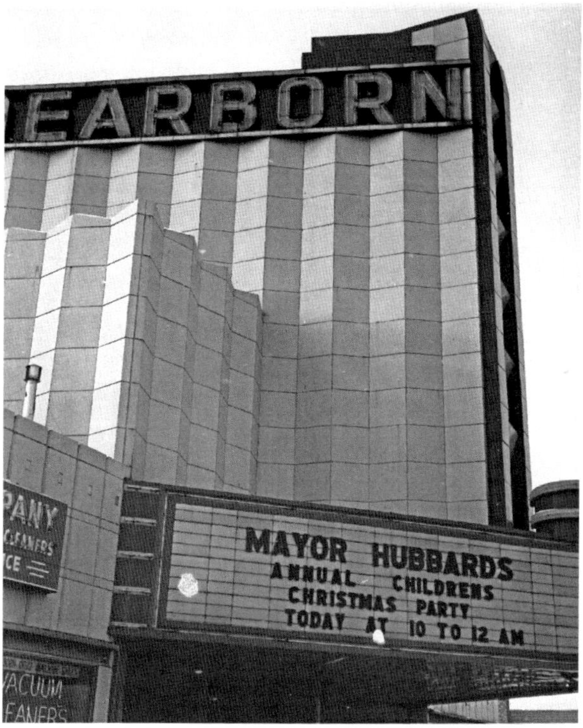

Charles N. Agree designed a new movie house that was built and opened in 1941. It was called the Dearborn Theater and was originally a one-screen theater. In later years, it was carved up into multiple theaters. *Dearborn Historical Museum.*

the Circle as well as the other area theaters such as the Carmen and Calvin. The students were allowed in for free and would be given a candy bar and admission into a movie. A theater company purchased the Circle Theater in the early 1960s. The new owners changed the name to the Camelot and transformed the look into a medieval style. The theater was purchased again in 1988, and the single auditorium was split into three. Declining business brought the closing of the Camelot in the mid-1990s. Over the years, the building has been remodeled to the point where it is no longer recognizable from its thriving movie-showing days.

In this same period when the design and construction of huge theaters really got rolling, a huge Charles N. Agree–designed movie house was built and opened in 1941. It was called the Dearborn Theatre and originally seated 1,498, all on one floor. Agree had also designed Detroit's famous Royal Theater, and his Dearborn structure was just a smaller version of the Royal. The structure embodied the bold Streamline Modern style and contained a small stage, but it had no dressing rooms or orchestra pit. In the late 1960s, a small three-hundred-seat auditorium was added and dubbed the Dearborn Living Room. A third screen was added in the 1970s. In the

1980s, the huge auditorium was carved up into multiple theaters. In 1992, Showcase Cinemas took over the Dearborn, and it was renamed Showcase Cinemas Dearborn. This venue remained popular for several years until the early 2000s, when patrons began looking elsewhere for their entertainment sources. It closed in 2006 and was razed in 2010.

The list of Dearborn movie theaters stands as a testament to the many smiling faces that were thrilled to fill up these structures week after week: the Alden, Calvin, Carmen, Camelot, Circle, Congress, Dearborn, Ford Grand, Fordson, Midway, the Ray and Strand—just to name a few—a tribute to a time when being a guest at a theater was something special and Dearborn was as taken with the phenomenon as the rest of the country was.

5

WHERE WE USED TO EAT, DRINK (AND SOMETIMES SLEEP)

The concept of the restaurant began in eighteenth-century France. When thousands of chefs who once serviced the aristocratic and royal households found themselves unemployed after the French Revolution, they turned to a new idea that we call today the restaurant experience. Of course, this whole business model took some time to take hold in different parts of the world. The development usually had to do with need or convenience or a combination of the two. In the case of an area like Dearborn, in the early days when settlers were coming from the East, the need for a place to grab some refreshment and lodging arose immediately. These early establishments on the frontier were called taverns. Taverns satisfied the demands and needs of travelers as they attempted to get from one place to another and especially serviced the special situation that existed in this area of large groups of people who were migrating to new lands.

One of the first taverns erected in the area was the Ten Eyck Tavern. Conrad Ten Eyck, one of the earliest European settlers to the area, moved to Dearborn in 1823 and quickly saw the need for travelers to be "helped on their way," as he put it. So, with this in mind, in 1826, he built the Ten Eyck Tavern on the south side of the Chicago Road (today Michigan Avenue) near the Rouge River and what would become the entrance to the Henry Ford Estate. The timing could not have been better, as the Erie Canal had just been completed in 1825 and travelers who had reached Detroit could reach the tavern with an intense day's journey along the Chicago Road. Much of that journey was through the woods, and when they arrived, the wagons would be parked in a yard area. For those who had a covered wagon, the men would take shelter there while the women and children would enter the tavern for the warm comfort of the fire. It has been recorded that the location was so crowded at times that there were many who had to sleep on the floor. In terms of food, everyone who entered was served either woodchuck hash or wolf steak. Legend has it that Michigan received its nickname "Wolverine State" at Ten Eyck Tavern because when patrons were told they were going to be eating wolf steak, they would respond that eating wolf must make them "wolverines." When the railroad was completed in 1837, it transported people past the tavern. Conrad Ten Eyck saw the amount of travel by wagon and stagecoach rapidly decrease, and the establishment closed. The structure was used to store grain until 1885, when it burned down. Ten Eyck died in 1847, and his large land holdings were passed onto his sons, who later sold the acreage to Henry Ford. It would be just a short distance away from where the tavern stood that Ford would build his Fair Lane estate.

Another early tavern that is definitely worthy of discussion was built in 1829. Built on the north side of the Chicago Road near Oakwood Boulevard, Thompson's Tavern was a welcome sight to those looking for a warm place to sleep and some refreshment. Many of those seeking food and shelter here had just passed the Ten Eyck Tavern but were forced to go a bit farther due to overcrowding. Built only a few years before the construction of the Detroit Arsenal at Dearbornville, it was perfectly positioned to service not only weary travelers but also the soldiers who were stationed at the arsenal. Although the structure would be short-lived, the way in which it met its demise was anything but customary. By 1837, a dispute over the ownership of the land that the tavern occupied was ready to boil over. Joshua Howard, who had been first commandant of the arsenal and by 1837 was serving as the sheriff of Wayne County, and the U.S. government both claimed ownership. On August 4, 1837, the new commandant of the Detroit Arsenal, Captain Webb, was given a court order to tear down Thompson's Tavern. Howard and a few men he had gathered together met Captain Webb and arsenal soldiers near the tavern. Howard was intent on protecting his land claim. A battle ensued, and one of the combatants was killed as a result. In the end, Captain Webb attained his objective, which was the razing of Thompson's Tavern.

Having served such a necessary role in the establishment of the Dearborn area, two other taverns are worthy of note. Built in 1864 by Joseph Schaefer on what is today the northeast corner of Michigan Avenue and Schaefer Road, the Schaefer Six Mile House became well

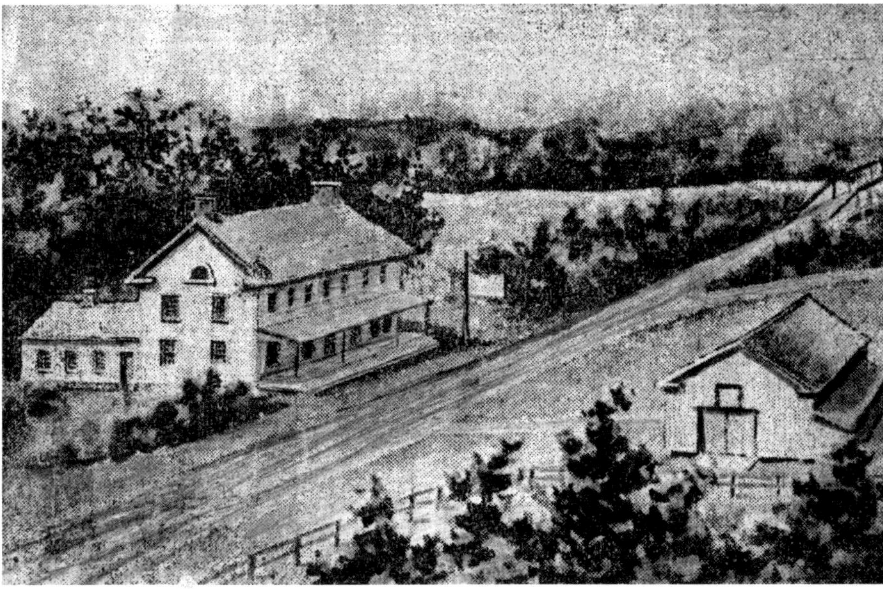

The Ten Eyck Tavern, built in 1826, would have been a welcome sight for weary travelers coming down the Chicago Road (Michigan Avenue) and close to the Rouge River. *Dearborn Historical Museum.*

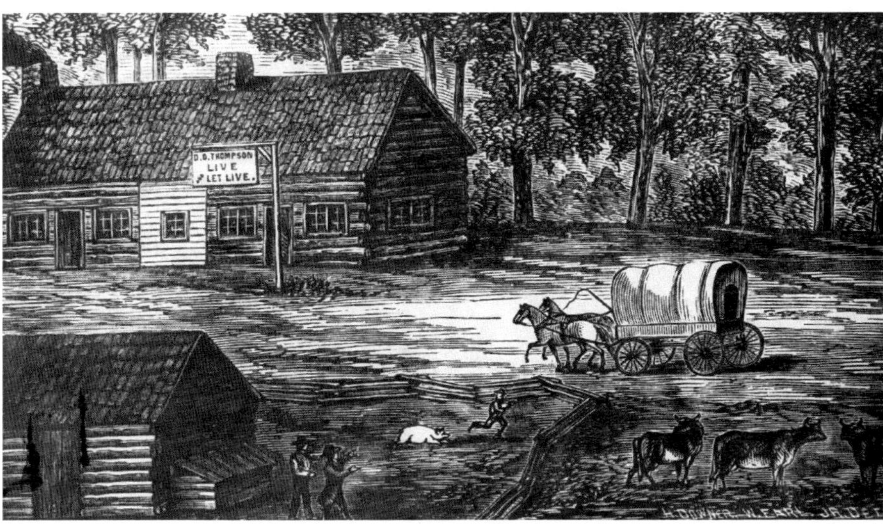

Built on the north side of the Chicago Road near Oakwood Boulevard in 1829, Thompson's Tavern was perfectly positioned to service weary travelers and soldiers who would be stationed at the arsenal in a few years. *Dearborn Historical Museum.*

known in a short amount of time. Schaefer foresaw the need for an inn where weary travelers could stop, rest and recharge before continuing their rugged stagecoach journey over rut-filled roads. Eventually, a grocery store was added, and hay scales at the house were used by farmers to weigh cattle, hogs and hay. On the second floor of the structure, there was a dance hall where social events could take place on special occasions. As was the custom in early taverns, meals were free. Schaefer and his crew would serve up food such as bean soup, sauerkraut, biscuits, vegetables and crackers. Oftentimes, these early establishments were given a mile moniker in their name to denote how far they were from a set base. In this case, it was the Six Mile House because it was six miles from the Detroit City Hall. In later years, this establishment was operated by Joseph's son, John, and the business continued until 1918. In 1929, John decided to carry on the legacy of progress that his family had become known for and that had been well established by his father and grandfather. He leveled the old inn and broke ground for a new structure: a massive granite and terra-cotta retail and office complex in a modern art deco style.

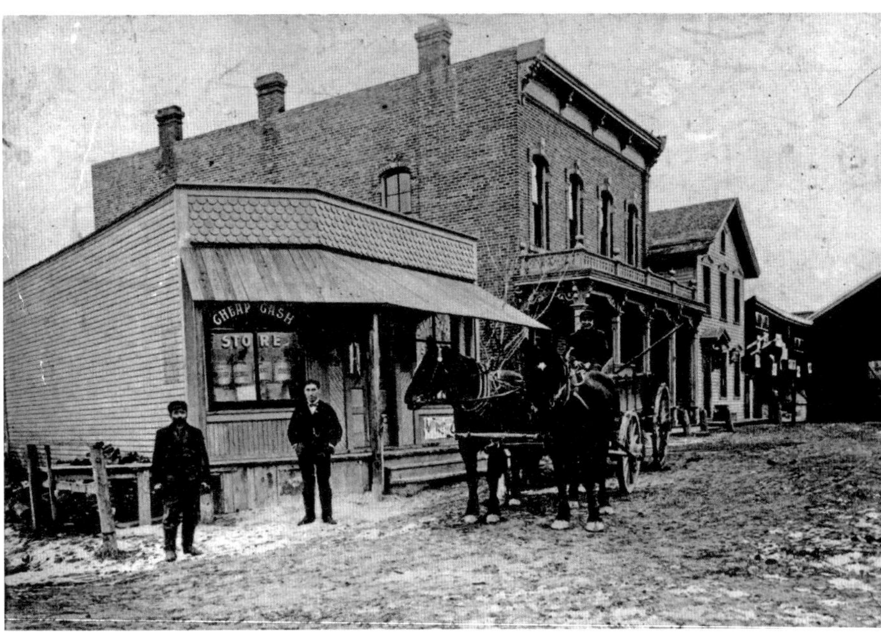

Joseph Schaefer started this establishment in 1864. Known as the Schaefer Six Mile House, it provided a place to rest and recharge with some food and drink. *Dearborn Historical Museum.*

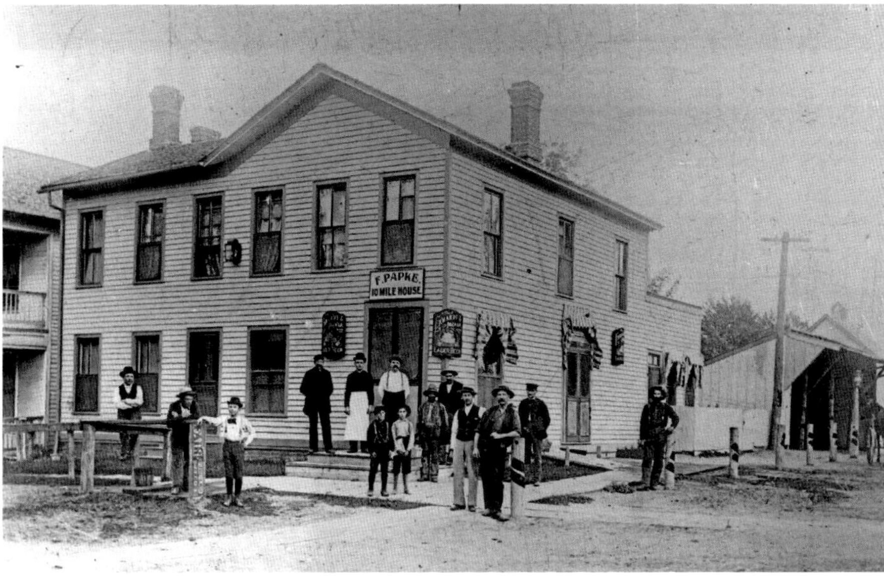

Papke's Tavern was located on what is today the southeast corner of Michigan Avenue and Monroe. Meals were free, and the latest news and gossip flowed freely. *Dearborn Historical Museum.*

The Papke Tavern, or Ten Mile House, was located farther west on what is today the southeast corner of Michigan Avenue and Monroe Street. Again, as was the custom in many taverns, meals were free if you were renting a room, and there was always an opportunity to catch up on the latest news or gossip. This establishment burned down in 1900. Another tavern was built on the same spot that would later be incorporated into Kiernan's Steakhouse. After the fire, the Papke family owned Papke's Sample Room on the northwest corner of Michigan Avenue and Monroe Street. While long gone now, history marks these businesses for having served such an important function in the days of the pioneers and stagecoach travel.

While the tavern setup worked well, there came a time in the latter 1800s when the word *hotel* became closely associated with a place to find first-class lodging, and the tavern went the way of a place more closely linked with the consumption of spirits. The Dearborn Hotel was built on the southwest corner of Michigan Avenue and Monroe Street in the 1830s. It was a large two-story structure that served its purpose of providing lodging for weary travelers. It remained in operation until March 31, 1896, when it burned to the ground. Anthony Wagner and his son Charles realized that Dearborn needed a first-rate hotel, and they built the Wagner Hotel on the same spot.

Anthony had solidified a great reputation as a brick maker, and when he moved to Dearborn Township, he established his own brickyards just off of Oakwood Boulevard and just south of Michigan Avenue. He was well known for making quality bricks, and many Wagner bricks were used to build fine Dearborn homes as well as Saint Joseph's Retreat and Eloise. When the decision was made to build a hotel, the original design called for two floors with a third-floor ballroom, but the third floor never materialized. Construction occurred at a furious pace, and it was ready for operation just prior to Christmas 1896. The twenty-eight-room structure was built with bricks from the Wagner brickyard. A large water tank on the roof supplied running water to the patrons. Beginning in the 1930s, the hotel became more of a boardinghouse, and the first floor was used by a variety of businesses, including a smoke shop, a candy store and a drugstore. The property was shut down completely in 1969. Ford Motor Company is presently moving forward with plans to invest in the entire block, and the structure will receive new life while maintaining its historic façade. It is being renovated into retail and office space as part of the planned development.

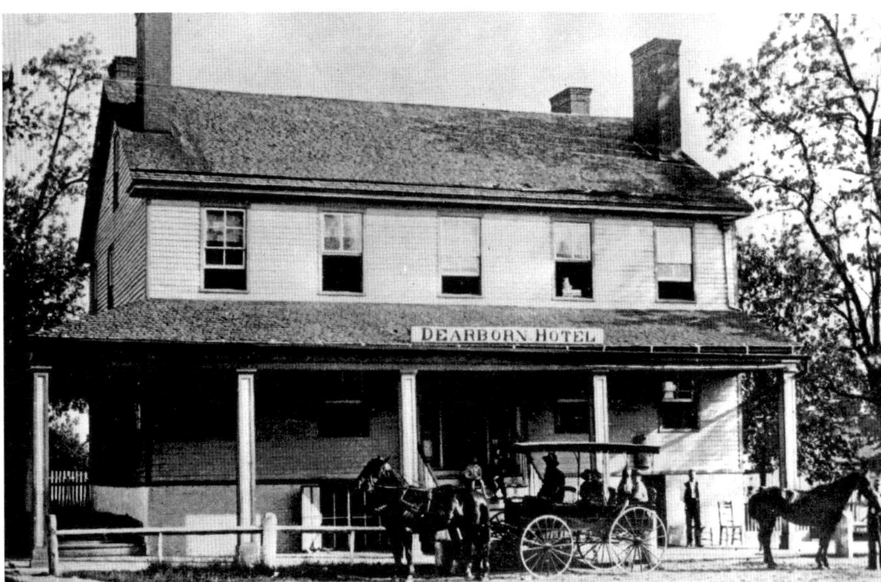

The Dearborn Hotel was built on the southwest corner of Michigan Avenue and Monroe in the 1830s. It burned to the ground in 1896, and the Wagner Hotel was built on the same land. *Dearborn Historical Museum.*

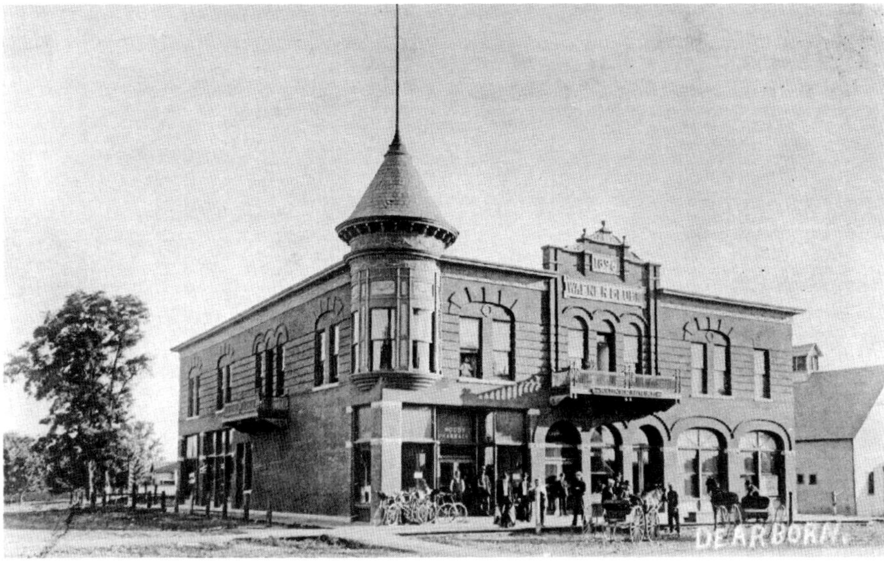

Erected in 1896 by Anthony Wagner and his son Charles, this twenty-eight-room hotel was made from bricks that came from the Wagner brickyard. The building still stands and is a testament to Dearborn's legacy of hospitality. *Dearborn Historical Museum.*

As Dearborn began to move into the more modern era of motels, sleek-looking structures like the Fairlane Inn were built. Completed in 1959 at Michigan Avenue and Brady Street, the motel experienced tremendous popularity for a number of years. The Fairlane Inn also has a secret past that many readers might not be aware of. In 1961, the conference room on the second floor was used by then Ford Motor Company vice president Lee Iacocca and other senior Ford executives for secret meetings related to the development of a cutting-edge vehicle that Ford believed had the potential to be a top seller. That vehicle would become known as the Ford Mustang. After the motel fell on hard times, much of it was demolished in 2010 except for one section that is now being used by the Dearborn Historical Museum for storage.

The twentieth century brought tremendous change as more and more people became residents and the area became more established. Less out of necessity and more out of providing individual service, new touches became an integral part in establishments that began to dot the area. For instance, guests were no longer required to sit at a common table as was the case in most taverns. Guests could now enjoy a meal at their own private tables. There were only a small number of restaurants early on as residents

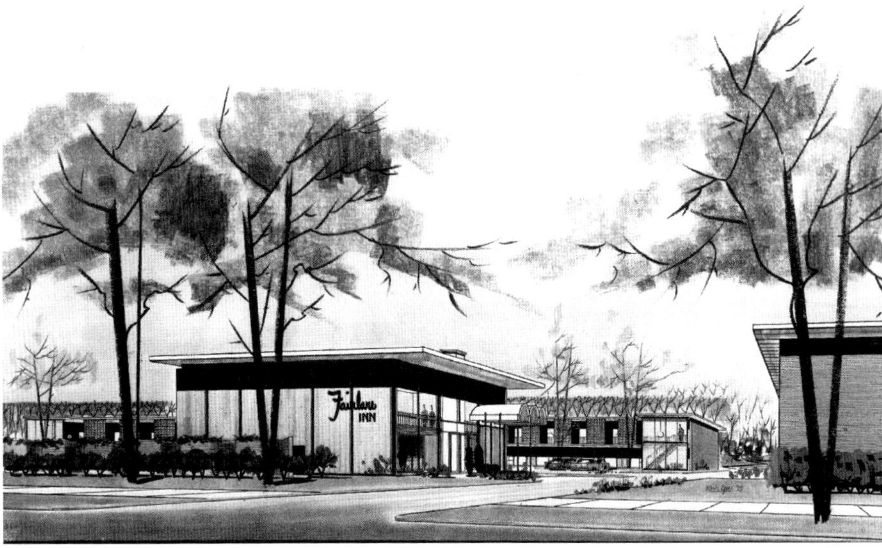

Built during a more modern era when sleek-looking motels were all the rage, the Fairlane Inn was completed in 1959 at the corner of Michigan Avenue and Brady Street. *Dearborn Historical Museum.*

who made the area their home for the most part prepared and consumed food and drink there. But as the twentieth century progressed, marketing and the needs and demands of families changed, and a wide variety of eating establishments popped up all over Dearborn. Included in this, of course, was a new concept: franchise restaurants. Residents and visitors of Dearborn have seen a little bit of everything in terms of dining variety. Some of these establishments became more than just popular eateries; they became institutions and gained a special place in the hearts of Dearbornites. And even though they are long gone, they live on in the hearts and minds of those who loved each and every experience.

The citizens of Dearborn and area residents have had the opportunity to experience everything from fine-dining establishments to venues like hamburger joints and drive-ins. One of the most popular drive-ins to ever grace Dearborn was called the Sip 'N' Nip. Built in the 1940s on the northeast corner of Telegraph and Sheridan, there was only walk-in and drive-up service available. Telegraph at the time was only four lanes, and there was no median. Nicknamed the "Sip" by regular patrons, the menu was full of the usual suspects, which were consistently cooked to perfection: hamburgers, hotdogs and grilled cheese. But what made the experience at the Sip 'N' Nip even more special was the variety of shakes and malts. Drive-in service called for the headlights to be on. Carhops would deliver orders. It was a popular spot after a movie or game and certainly a date night kind of a place. Custom cars made regular stops at the Sip 'N' Nip, and it was home to several car clubs. It was torn down in 1959 when Telegraph was widened.

Another location that many Dearbornites became attached to when it was time to grab a burger was Powers Hamburgers. Started in 1935, regulars claimed the burgers rivaled Miller's. Located at Michigan Avenue and Oakwood Boulevard, it didn't matter whether a patron sat at the counter or in the one booth, taste buds were in for a real treat. The building was torn down in 1999.

Quite a different pace and décor could be found at the Woodworth House. Built in 1840 by Alfred Woodworth, a wealthy agriculturist, as a

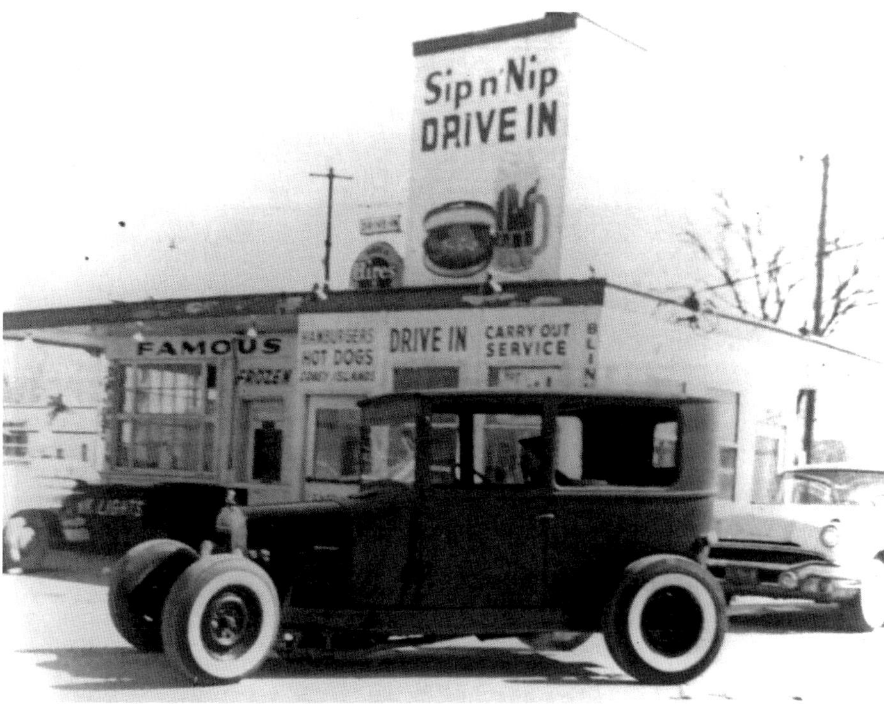

The 1940s and 1950s brought a car culture that called for a special eating establishment. The Sip 'N' Nip epitomized such a place, with carhops and exceptional hamburgers and shakes. *Dearborn Historical Museum.*

dwelling for his family, the last resident died, leaving the future of the building uncertain. Roy Lancaster rented the structure and operated it as a restaurant for many years. Patrons were always enthralled by the bar area and the player piano. And many a senior prom dinner was hosted by the Woodworth House. There was certainly an air of sophistication with the white tablecloths and professional service staff. The unique and elegant experience ended in 1979 when the landlord refused to renew the lease. There was quite a fight to save the building by a preservation group—but to no avail. In 1981, the historic Woodworth House at Michigan Avenue and Ternes Street was torn down to make way for a Burger King.

For lovers of hats and fine dining, the Topper was always a destination worth visiting. Founded in the early 1940s and located at Michigan Avenue and Oakwood Boulevard, the walls were filled with framed photographs of famous and not-so-famous people donning headwear. There were pictures of Charlie Chaplin and Winston Churchill in bowlers, Humphrey Bogart and Frank Sinatra in fedoras, John Wayne and Randolph Scott in Stetsons. The owners, George and Tony Koustas, were always walking around in bucket hats to check on the satisfaction level of the customers. In addition to this unique atmosphere, the food and drinks were among the best in the

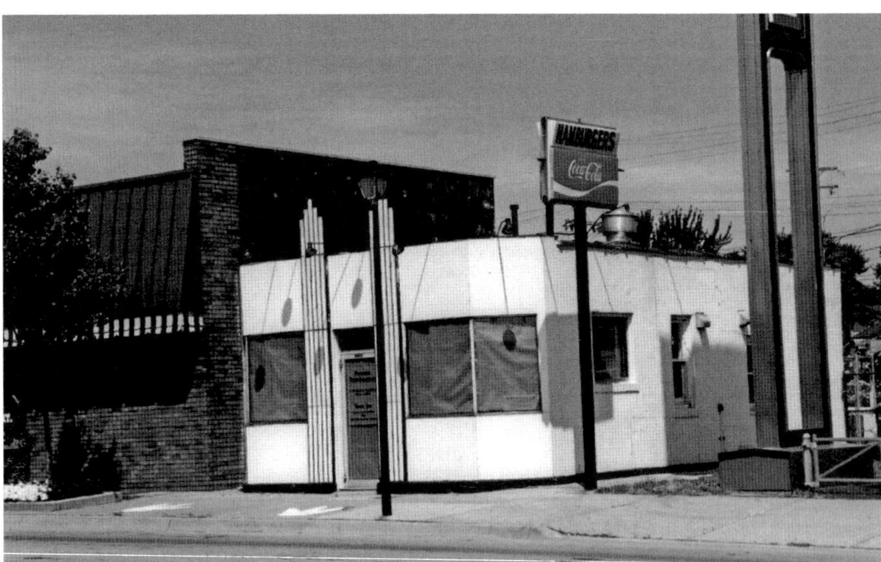

Patrons' taste buds would wait in great anticipation at Powers Hamburgers. Started in 1935, many a tasty hamburger was served up at Michigan Avenue and Oakwood Boulevard. *Dearborn Historical Museum.*

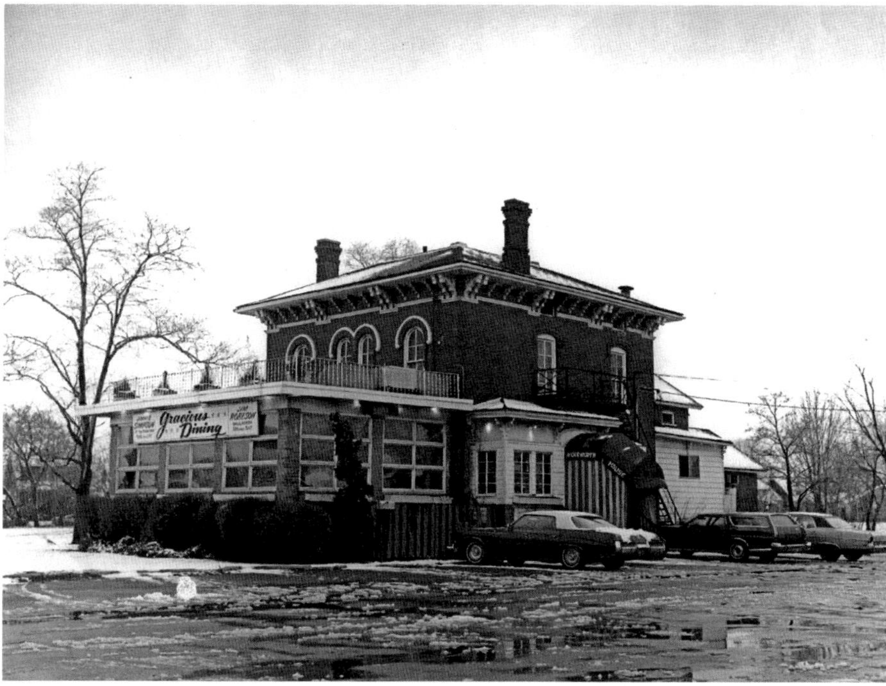

Originally built in 1840 by Alfred Woodworth for his family, this structure was turned into an inviting dining establishment and served the community well until 1979. *Dearborn Historical Museum.*

entire area. The menu was filled with amazing choices, from braised short ribs to seafood. The bar area was lively and most of the time it was filled to capacity. In terms of drinks, the wine selection included quite a variety of choices: several chardonnays, cabernet sauvignon and merlot. The name of the establishment was changed to Tony K's Grill in 2001 and then it became Cheli's Chili Bar around 2003. Cheli's closed in 2013, and the location became known as the Nar Bar, which went out of business in 2016. The building is presently vacant.

Every respectable downtown must have an exceptional fish establishment, and the one that fit the bill perfectly for Dearborn was Meyers Seafood. Located across from the Calvin Theater, the restaurant opened in 1947. Known for its giant aquarium and red leather moon-shaped booths, one experience here and patrons knew they had been in the best seafood location in the area. Meyers became famous for some of the best lobster around Dearborn. It became Doug's Body Shop restaurant in 1976, and the building burned down the next year.

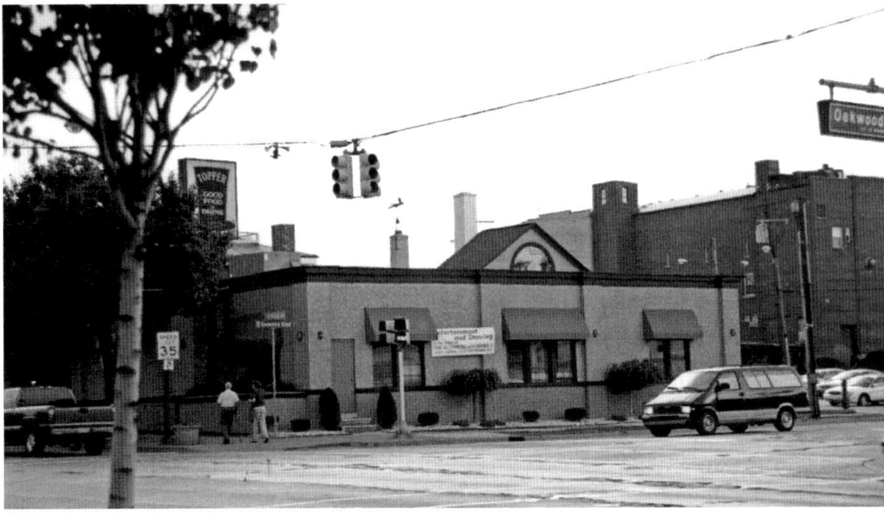

The Topper, located on the northwest corner of Michigan Avenue and Oakwood, was a destination in demand for many years because of its high-quality food and drink, atmosphere and excellent service. *Dearborn Historical Museum.*

Every city or town needs dining establishments that become places for regulars. One of the establishments in the area that fits this description and one of the best spots in Dearborn to grab a drink and enjoy perfectly cooked filet mignon was Kiernan's, the ultimate family-owned and operated business. The Kiernan family started the business in 1965 and eventually incorporated all of the buildings from 21931 to 21961 Michigan Avenue. This venue holds a special place in the hearts of many area residents. After several years of seeing business decline, Kiernan's closed in 2014. It was replaced by Liv lounge, which only lasted two years. The complex was torn down in 2017 to make way for a construction project spearheaded by Ford Motor Company. One of the finest cocktail lounges and dining rooms to ever grace the city of Dearborn was known as Baja's. Located at 23955 Michigan Avenue, Baja's opened in 1959 and offered live music by well-known local groups. Originally owned and operated by long-running Dearborn city councilman John Baja, the location went through many changes through the years and was eventually sold to Chuck Muer. The name changed to Sundog in 1969. The business was sold in 1975, then sold again the next year. In September 1980, new life was attempted as Baja's Place, but that only lasted a few years. By 1990, the building was vacant, and it has since been razed.

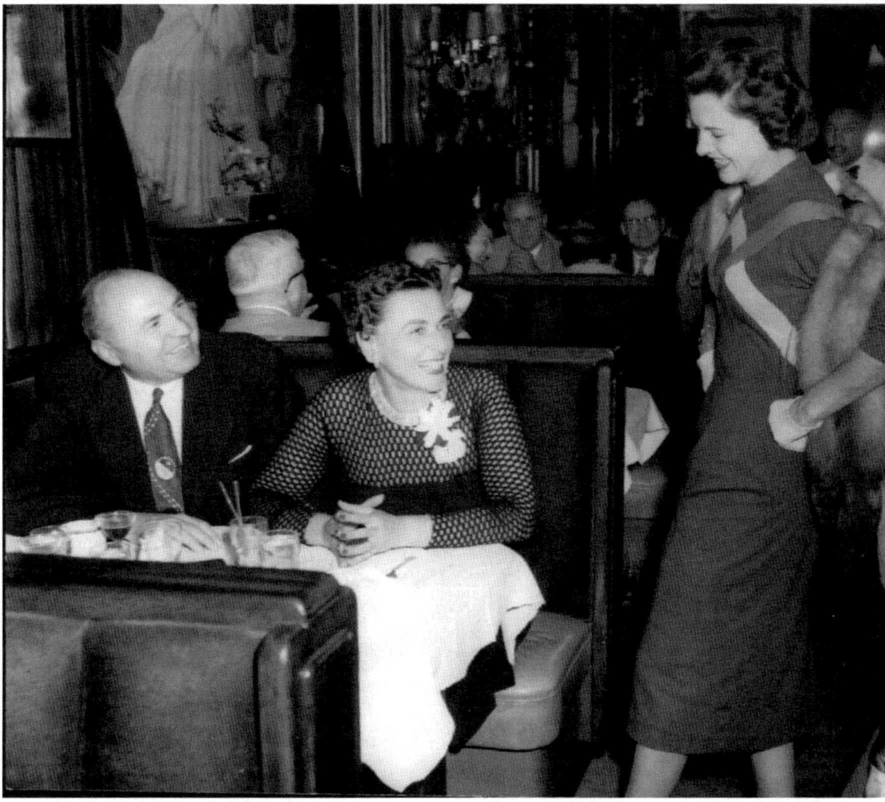

Every city needs a high-end seafood establishment, and Meyers Seafood Restaurant on Michigan Avenue and Howard certainly fit that bill and more. Seen here in 1957, Model Jan Nichols shows off her attire as diners look on. *Dearborn Historical Museum.*

Neighborhood bars have been the lifeblood of drinking and social life in Dearborn since the first half of the twentieth century. There are numerous examples that could be cited in the history of the area, but one of the best examples of this kind of establishment was Howell's Bar. The structure was originally located at 22093 Michigan Avenue and was known by the name Johnson's Restaurant, which was managed by Eunice Howell and began operating in 1941. The name changed to Johnson's Bar in 1943. The building was moved from Michigan Avenue in 1947 to make room for the construction of a Winkelman's store. The new address for the building became 1035 Mason Street, and the name was changed to Howell's Beer Garden in 1948. Known for its friendly atmosphere, Howell's was one of those places where patrons immediately felt at ease and could relax. The menu provided a nice selection of high-quality pub grub at very reasonable

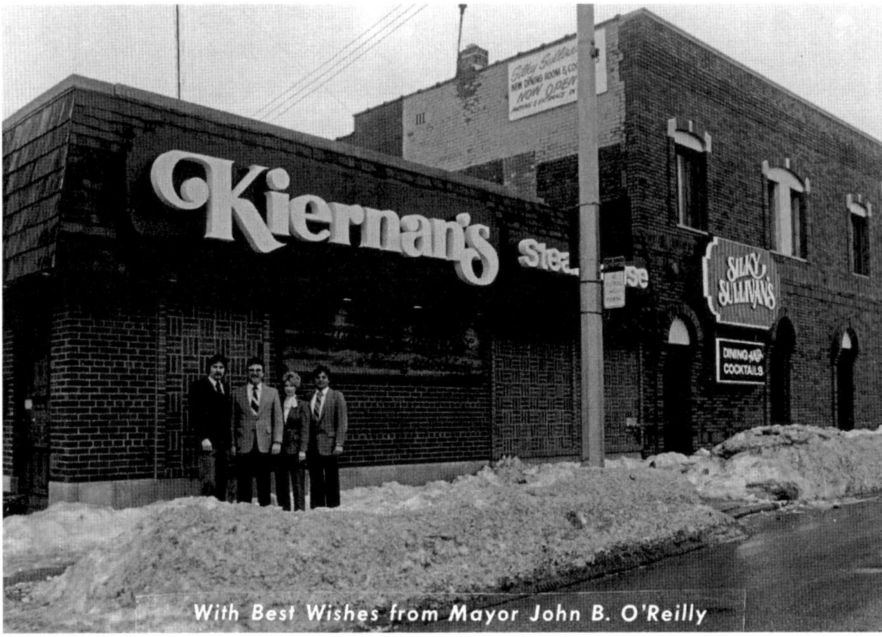

One of the best places in Dearborn to grab a drink and enjoy perfectly cooked filet mignon, Kiernan's was the ultimate family-owned and operated business. Pictured here are, *from left to right*: Kevin Kiernan, Terry Kiernan, Terry Donnely and Michael Ray, 1982. *Dearborn Historical Museum.*

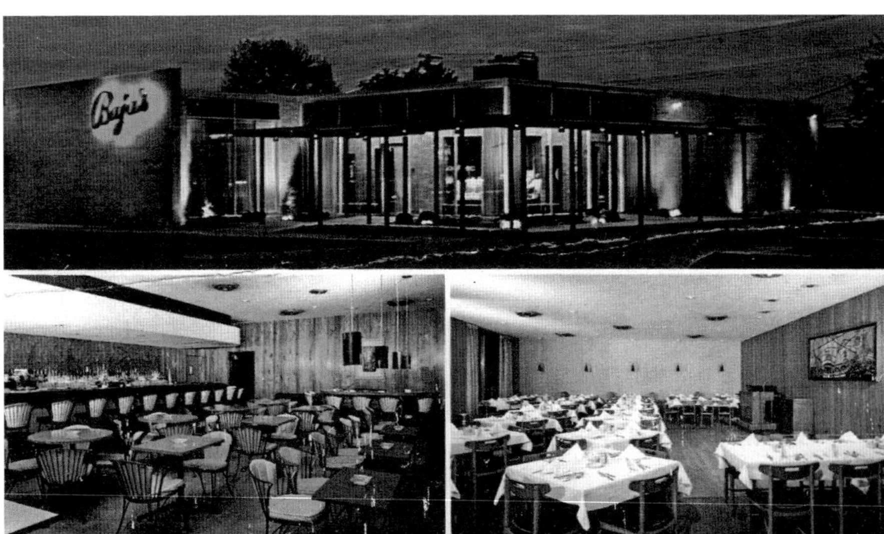

Pictured here in the 1960s, many who experienced this establishment would agree that Baja's was one of Dearborn's finest cocktail lounges and dining rooms. *Dearborn Historical Museum.*

prices. And the huge menu of beers would never disappoint, as there were many domestics as well as international varieties to pick from. The mixed drinks were crafted by quality bartenders and never watered down. A fire caused the business to close in 2014, and the structure was razed.

A fun atmosphere could always be expected at the Gas Buggy Cantina at 14628 Warren Avenue. Great food and even better drinks were always flowing at this establishment. Opened in 1971 as the Gas Buggy Lounge, it closed down in 1991. A commercial strip mall now exists on the site. One establishment that had a long run in Dearborn and definitely had something for everyone was Christoff's, located at 13736 Michigan Avenue. This unique venue meant different things to different people. For some, it was a neighborhood bar, and for others, it was more along the lines of fine dining. It opened in 1944 and operated until 1989. La Trattoria Italian restaurant opened at the location in 1992, and presently, Petit Café and Grill has set up shop in the building.

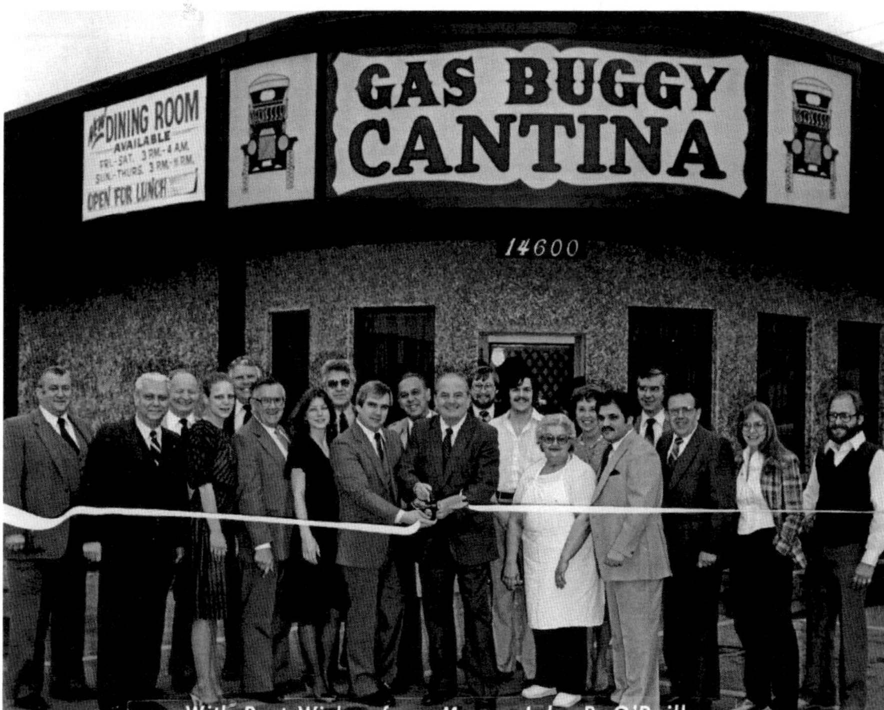

A fun atmosphere could always be expected at the Gas Buggy Cantina at 14600 Warren Avenue. Great food and even better drinks were always flowing at this establishment. *Dearborn Historical Museum.*

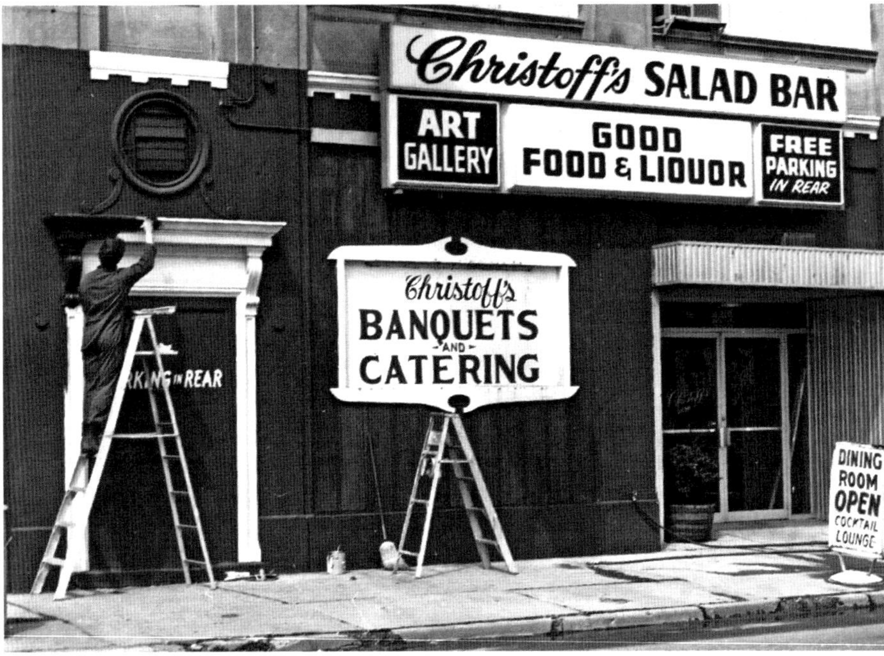

Christoff's, located at 13736 Michigan Avenue, meant different things to different people. For some, it was a neighborhood bar, and for others, it was more along the lines of fine dining. *Dearborn Historical Museum.*

And there is something else that truly makes Dearborn unique. The diversity that has always been a huge part of the community can be seen in the great variety of cuisine that has been made available to the residents and visitors through the years. To say that Dearborn has some of the absolute best Middle Eastern restaurants in the country would be stating a fact. And the diversity was stretched in another direction when Kyoto Japanese Steak House was added to the array of options in 1976. Located just outside of the Fairlane Town Center, at 18601 Hubbard Drive, the outside architecture featured a unique mansard roof, and the interior included a fascinating and specially built water wheel, which historically has been the center of attraction in the inns of Japan. The menu items were all prepared at each table by talented and entertaining Japanese chefs. This was definitely a happening establishment. The restaurant closed in the early 2000s, and the location is now a Benihana.

But there is much more to life than eating and drinking establishments. No respectable town or city should ever operate without a tasty sweet shop or confectionery. Dearborn has had many through the years. One was the

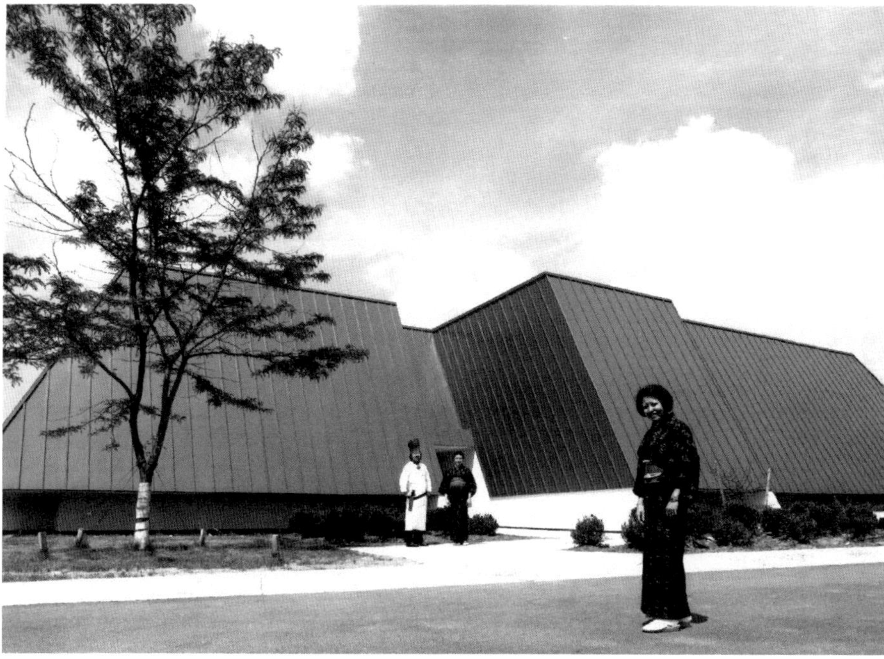

Having fun with food was always an option at Kyoto Japanese Steak House. Located at 18601 Hubbard Drive near Fairlane Town Center, meals were prepared right at each table by talented and entertaining Japanese chefs. *Dearborn Historical Museum.*

Calvin Sweet Shop, located on the ground floor of the Calvin Theater. Many fond memories were made here, as there was a jukebox, a snack bar menu complete with goodies and some intrigue. It became a regular haunt for students of Dearborn, Edsel Ford and Sacred Heart High Schools. There was a soda bar, a counter and booths. Couples would try to grab what they considered to be the best seats in the venue, which were the booths close to Michigan Avenue. Unfortunately, the building that housed the theater and the shops experienced several fires and had to close in 1981. And speaking of sweets, Sanders' had several locations in Dearborn, and each provided a chance for visitors to satisfy their need for something tasty. There were six Sanders' in Dearborn at various times, including locations at Michigan Avenue and Schaefer Road, Michigan Avenue and Mason Street and in the Westborn Shopping Center. Started by Fred Sanders in 1875 in Detroit, the locations became known for their delicious candy, fudge toppings and baked goods. They also offered light lunches and some tasty choices at their fountain counters, including ice cream sodas, sundaes and what they became famous for, hot fudge cream puffs. Another treat that Sanders' became known for

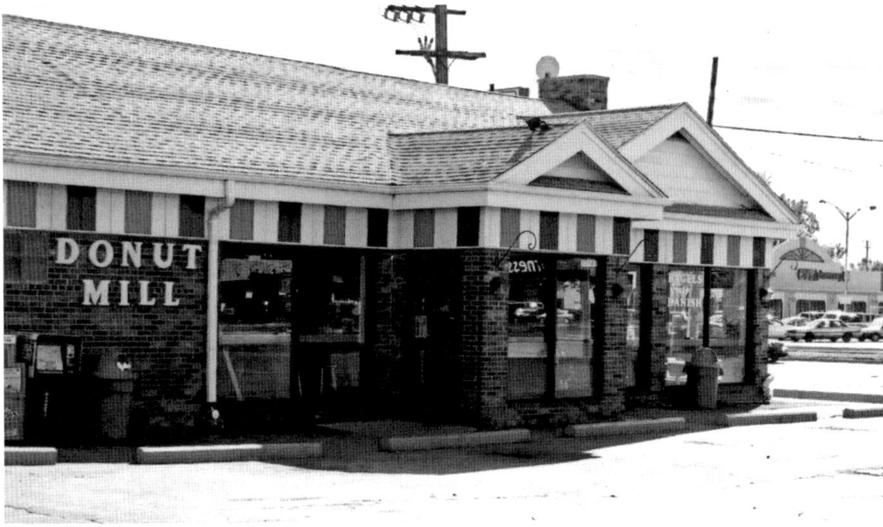

For twenty-four years, locals could not find a fresher donut than the Donut Mill at Michigan Avenue and Nowlin. Pictured here in 2002, it was a hangout for people employed in every vocation. Today, the structure is a Potbelly Sandwich. *Dearborn Historical Museum.*

through the years was the "Bumpy Cake," named for the chocolate ganache that covers thick ridges of buttercream. The location near Michigan Avenue and Schaefer Road opened in 1932 and closed in 1993. The location at Michigan Avenue and Mason Street started operations in 1948 and closed in 1982. And the Westborn store opened in 1959 and ceased operations around the year 2000. It has since been replaced by a post office outlet. In 2002, Morley Candy Company purchased Sanders, and a few retail outlets have sprung up around the metro Detroit area under the name that many Dearbornites still remember as bringing satisfaction to their sweet tooth.

One thing is certain: Dearborn has offered a wide array of very special and high-quality establishments through the years, and the tremendous variety has provided something for everyone. Whether seeking just a quick bite or a fine-dining experience or something in-between, the locations that have been covered in this chapter demonstrate an amazing heritage in this regard. And although Dearbornites can no longer frequent these venues, they speak to a wonderful legacy and no doubt many special memories. For those readers who patronized these establishments, this is a chance to reminisce. For those who are seeing them for the very first time, it is an opportunity to learn what Dearborn has offered throughout its history.

6

THE SHELVES ARE BARE

Few cities the size of Dearborn have had access to the wide variety of stores that the people of this area have. No matter what local residents have needed to purchase through the years, an establishment has arisen to fill the need. Whether it be a general store in the early days or high-quality retail of the second half of the twentieth century, the populace has been served by various businesses, many of which gained a place in the hearts and minds of those who frequented them. While communities are serviced by a wide array of service providers, this chapter will be limited to specific retail, including food-related operations.

As Dearborn grew, the need and demand for a variety of food items arose, and the general store—or in some cases small grocery stores—sprang up to provide what area shoppers needed. The G.C. Auten Grocery was just this kind of store. It was located on the northeast side of Michigan Avenue and Howard Street from 1916 to 1920. The Dearborn Post Office occupied the same structure. Mr. Auten was a village councilman, and Mrs. Auten was a substitute teacher at Dearborn Public Schools and assisted Dr. Foley, who had an office upstairs, administering anesthesia to patients. In later years, the building was occupied by Thieleman Drugs before becoming Brothers Tuxedo. Today, there is an empty lot where the building once stood. For a more specialized operation, a well-known family in the area, the Espers, ran a dairy operation that also delivered. The Esper farm was located on what is today Warren Avenue and Calhoun Street. The Esper Dearborn Dairy was located around the Michigan Avenue and Greenfield Road area and serviced not only Dearborn but also portions of west Detroit. As one of the early families to settle in the area, the Esper name became well known. Peter Esper and his family came to the area from Germany in 1842 and settled in what is known today as East Dearborn. The dairy operation began in 1886, and it closed around 1915 when the Esper farm was sold. The dairy delivery routes were sold to the Detroit Creamery.

When one considers Dearborn's diversity through the years, it should come as no surprise that specialty markets popped up all over the place. A good example of this is Trotta Brothers Market, which was located on the southwest corner of Schaefer Road and Ellar Street. The market initially opened in 1931 at 4431 Schaefer Road. After several successful years there, a new location was opened at 4423 Schaefer Road. It went out of business in 1947. The second location became the Parna Brothers Market in 1950 and then Alcamos Market in 1954. Alcamos is still going strong as of this writing. Meanwhile, during the same period over in West Dearborn, Isador

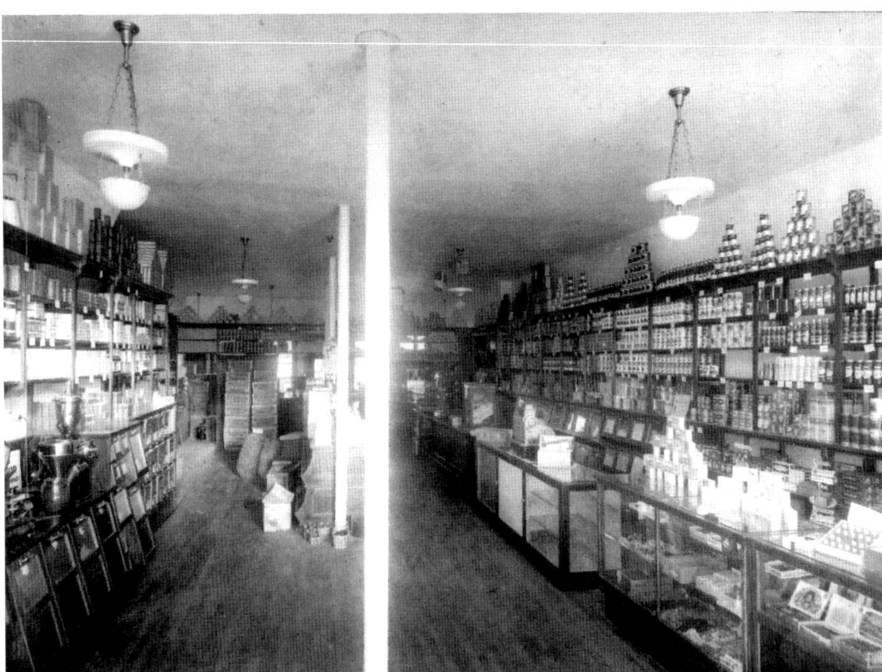

The G.C. Auten Grocery was located on the northeast side of Michigan and Howard. The store, pictured here in 1916, occupied the building until 1920. *Dearborn Historical Museum.*

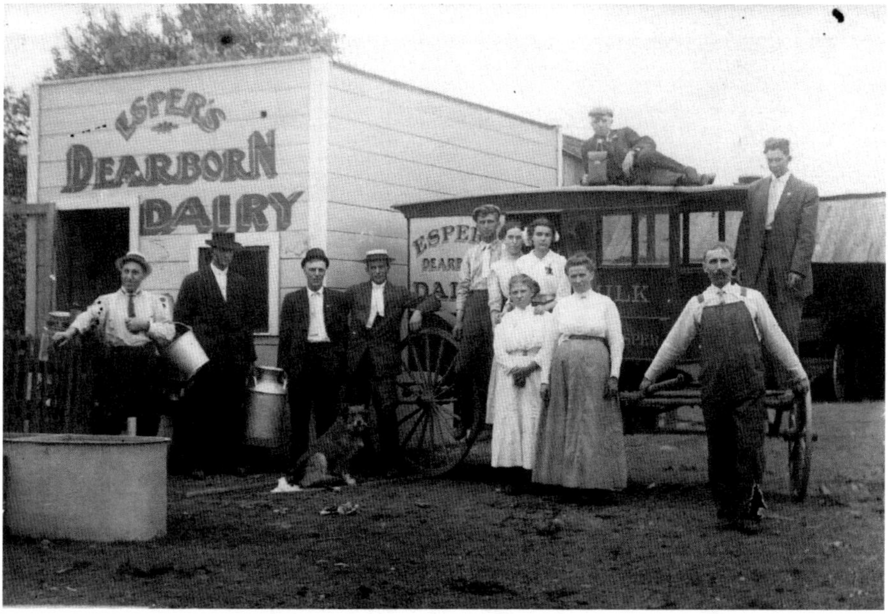

The Esper Dearborn Dairy, seen here in 1908, was located around the Michigan Avenue and Greenfield area and serviced not only Dearborn but also portions of west Detroit. Pictured here are, *from left to right*: Joseph Dornoff (shirt sleeves), Ben Theisen, Frank Dornoff, John Esper, Joseph Esper, Clara Esper, Mary Dornoff, unidentified, Ed Reuter (on wagon), Nora Esper, Mary Esper and Henry Esper. *Dearborn Historical Museum.*

Strub purchased what was known as the Dearborn Public Market from David Newman in 1942. The business was located at 22065 Michigan Avenue. Strub had opened his first meat market in East Dearborn in 1916. And during the Depression, he employed people and gave food on credit to those who were hurting to the point where he almost went bankrupt himself. During World War II, he charged twenty-five cents a pound for pot roast and thirty-three cents for two pounds of ham. Strub's claim to fame is that he was Dearborn's only cowboy, as at the age of seventeen he mounted a horse and drove cattle right down Michigan Avenue. Strub sold the business in 1963, and the location went out of business in 1973. The building's most recent occupant was the Post Bar, which is now closed.

Dearborn has had many furniture stores over the years. One of these operations included two different businesses located under the same roof. The Daly brothers established a furniture and mortuary business in 1917 on the south side of Michigan Avenue between Howard Street and Tenny Street. In 1974, Jacobson's purchased the building, and it became the

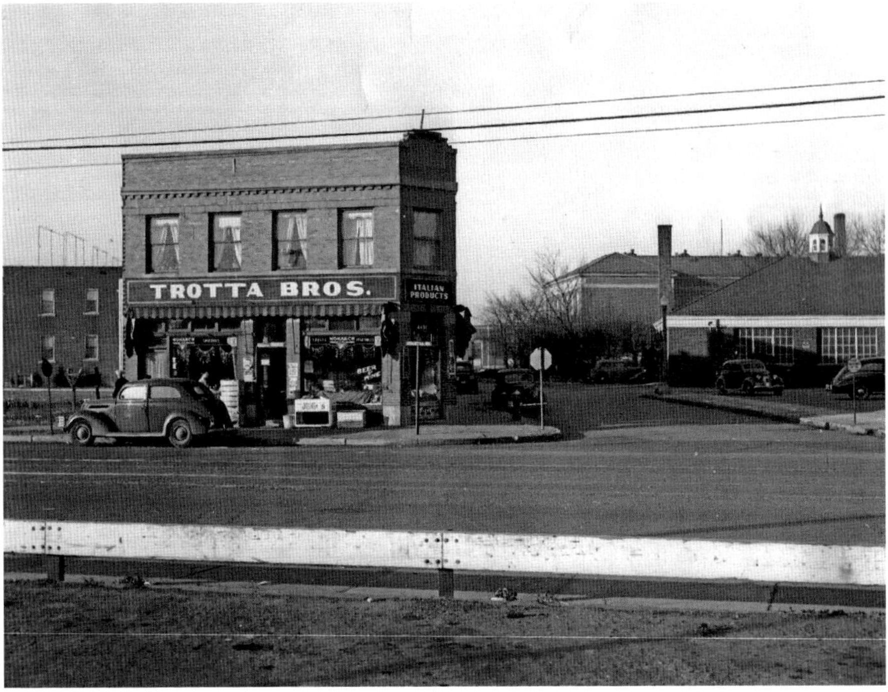

Trotta Bros. Market, shown here in 1940, was located on the southwest corner of Schaefer and Ellar in the shadow of city hall. The building still stands and now houses the Factory Finish Western Store. *Dearborn Historical Museum.*

Jacobson's Store for the Home. For specialty pieces, one would venture into Eurich's Furniture at 22266 Michigan Avenue. Established in the 1950s, there was a general store attached that included an old-fashioned soda emporium and a time travel experience back to the 1890s. Today, many have fond memories of the penny candy, Vermont cheddar cheese and Salem crackers and scrumptious dill pickles in the barrel. Patrons could also find a large variety of antiques and one of the world's largest collections of Colonial furniture. Other furniture options through the years included Dearborn Furniture at 13939 Michigan Avenue, which eventually became Robinson Furniture. Dearborn Furniture opened in 1948 and operated for twenty years until it was purchased by Robinson Furniture. Robinson operated for a few years until it became a warehouse store in 1973. Today, the building is used by more than one business, including the Detroit Jiu-Jitsu Academy and the Deals for Less Clothing Outlet.

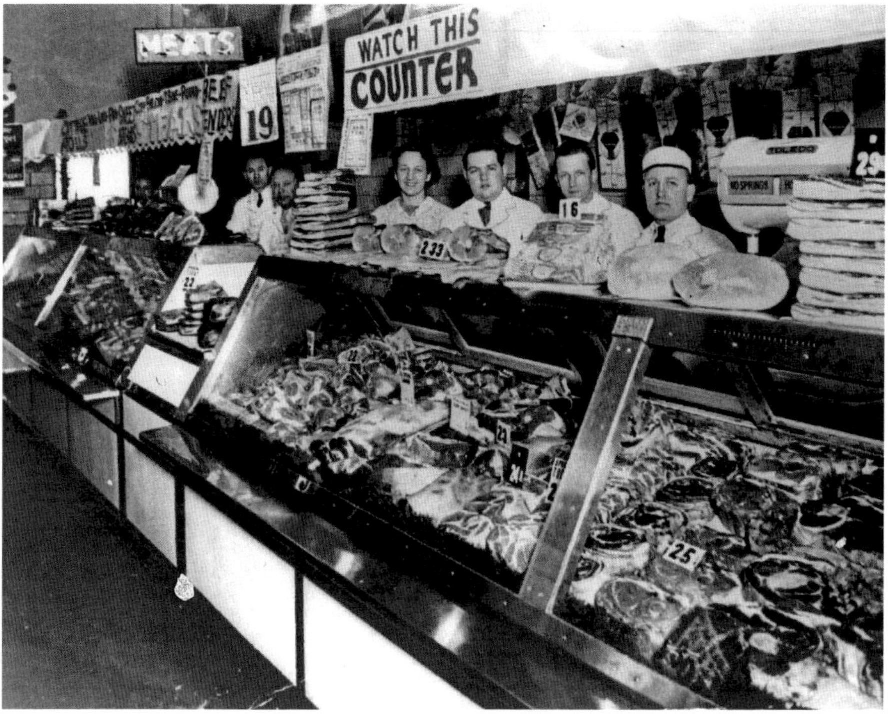

The Dearborn Public Market was located on the south side of Michigan Avenue between Monroe and Mason. It provided residents not just meat but a memorable experience. *Dearborn Historical Museum.*

Dearborn has had its fair share of iconic retail establishments throughout its history. In 1928, one of the few remaining structures from the days of the Detroit Arsenal, the saddler's shop, was torn down to make way for an S.S. Kresge store. The S.S. stood for the founder's first and middle names, which were Sebastian Stanley. Kresge arrived in Detroit in 1899, and all of the stores that he eventually established were of the five-and-dime variety, which were fast replacing the general or mercantile stores of earlier years. Located on Michigan Avenue near Monroe Street, this was one of many Kresge locations that would exist in Dearborn. This particular store is especially remembered fondly for its ham-and-cheese subs or roast beef sandwiches for forty cents, a fish dinner for fifty cents and everything was served at the lunch counter as patrons sat on stools that would swing all the way around. The fountain area was a very popular attraction for patrons who just wanted something special to drink. One glance at the menu and excellent options like malted milk shakes for twenty-five cents or a hot fudge sundae for twenty

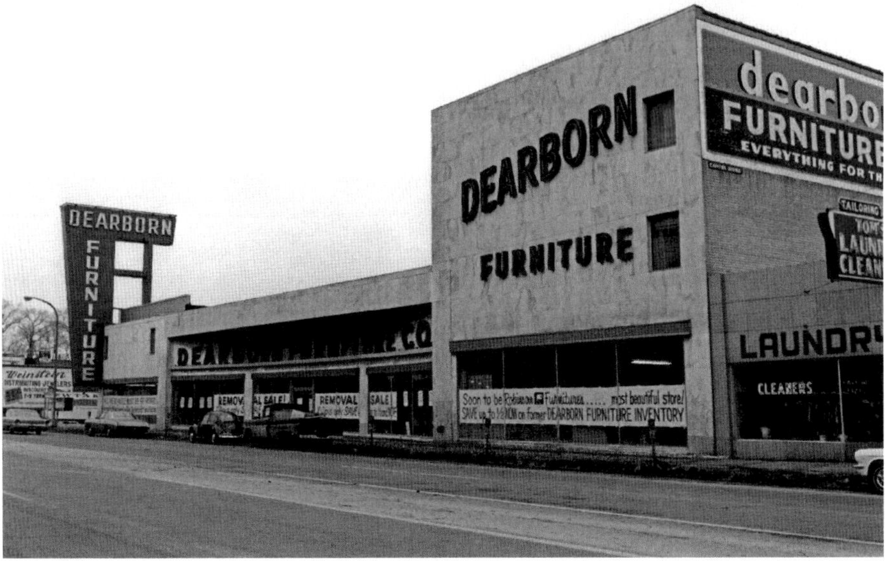

Dearborn has had many furniture stores through the years, and the building at 13939 Michigan Avenue housed both Dearborn Furniture and Robinson Furniture. Today, the structure is home to Detroit Jiu-Jitsu Academy and other outlets. *Dearborn Historical Museum.*

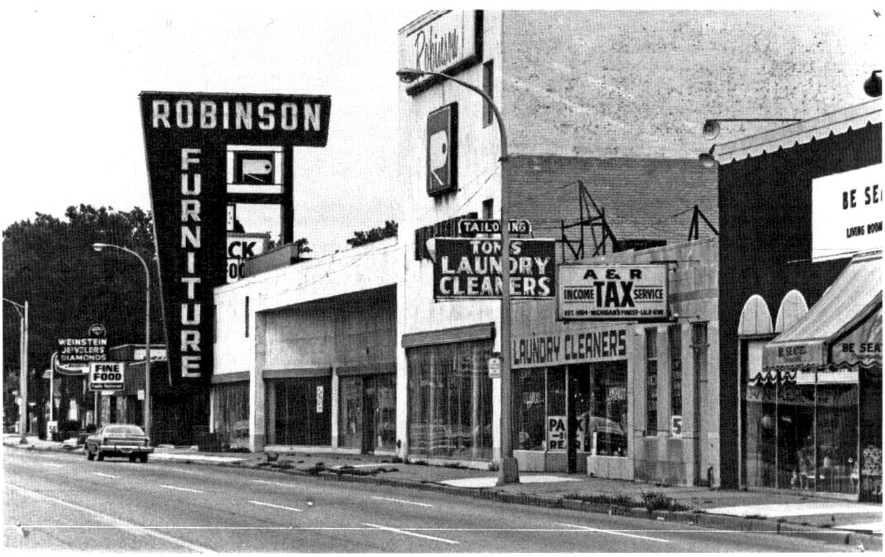

Continuing the tradition of offering furniture at this location, Robinson Furniture picked up the mantle in the late 1960s and operated until 1973, when a warehouse store moved in. *Dearborn Historical Museum.*

cents would present themselves. After a treat, customers could peruse a little bit of everything on the open counters. Whether a patron was looking for clothing, toys, candy, perfume, shaving lotion or anything else, the store was known for friendly and knowledgeable service. Whatever a shopper was in need of, there is a very good chance that it could be found at Kresge. By the 1970s, the popularity of the five-and-dime started to wane, and this location closed in 1973. A mini-mall moved into the building, but a fire destroyed the structure in 1976.

Montgomery Ward was a hub of activity for many years on the corner of Michigan Avenue and Schaefer Road. Begun as a mail-order business in 1872, in 1926, a transition began when the first retail store was opened. The Dearborn store opened in 1937, and it eventually expanded to ninety-three thousand square feet. The structure took up an entire city block. The complex had a very distinctive look and was constructed in Georgian style architecture. Ward's went through a period where management was looking for a consistent look on the exterior of their stores and they desired something that looked rich and elegant. In order to try to keep up with Sears, Ward's launched a frantic store construction program. There were 36 stores at the end of 1927. The company opened 208 more stores the following year and another 288 in 1929. Ward's went from having no stores to over 500 in just over three years. It did not take long to see that this was just too much growth in a short period of time. But once management was able to catch up by hiring exceptional talent, the retailer began to hit on some real success. It was during this period that the Dearborn location was built. Two years after the Dearborn store went up, in 1939, Montgomery Ward would make one of the most enduring contributions to America's pop culture heritage. A Ward's advertising copywriter named Robert L. May was assigned to put together a giveaway booklet for the stores to hand out as a Christmas promotion. He came up with a humorous twist on Clement Clark Moore's "The Night Before Christmas"—only in this booklet, a ninth reindeer was added to lead the pack that would pull Santa's sleigh and his name was Rudolph the Red-Nosed Reindeer. It was an instant hit. Years later, Ward's transferred the rights to the story to May, whose brother-in-law was Johnny Marks. Marks then wrote the famous song based on this version of the story. Gene Autry recorded the resulting hit. Patrons who entered the doors knew that browsing at Montgomery Ward was always going to be an experience, as there were so many different departments to visit, including electronics, appliances, clothes for every member of the family and for every occasion, purses, toys, a snack bar, tools, sporting goods, furniture and more.

Smelling the roasted peanuts as soon as the front door opened is something patrons came to expect. There was a charm school offered by the name of "Wendy Wards," where ladies could learn proper etiquette. And as an added bonus, customers could have their vehicle worked on in the auto repair garage while they got their shopping done. The doors closed for good in 2001. In 2008, the building was razed, and a multiuse structure that includes many healthcare-related entities was built on the spot.

In 1937, yet another retail player set up shop in Dearborn. Federals Department store was completed that year at 13624 Michigan Avenue. In the early 1960s, the store moved to Schaefer Road. The Michigan Avenue location then became Leeds Furniture, and today, the Arab American National Museum occupies the location. It was not uncommon for patrons to enter the store and make a beeline for the snack bar. The legend of the amazing Sloppy Joes made there still lives on to this day. The rumor that started to get around town that Federals offered absolutely everything was not far off base. And in addition to offering everything in terms of products, the store also offered modeling lessons. The chain filed for bankruptcy in 1972, and the Dearborn location closed in the mid-1970s.

In 1964, something very special happened in Dearborn with the construction of the tenth store in Jacobson's chain. Located on the south side of Michigan Avenue at Howard Street, it was built on the original location of Christ Episcopal Church. Jacobson's management stated at the time of its building that Dearborn was chosen because of the city's "world famous reputation as a vacation and tourist center and its desirable location and the availability of personnel." Jacobson's was always known for its high-quality merchandise and impeccable service. Ladies could make a day of it between shopping, eating at the Terrace Room or having their hair worked on in the salon. Management placed a premium on customer service. Sales staff would get to know customers in a much more personal way than is the case in most stores today. Relationships were formed between staff and customers to the point where patrons' individual styles were remembered by specific sales clerks. When styles arrived that meshed with a particular customer's likes, a call would be made to that customer informing them of the styles that had just arrived. The store even offered a charm school where proper etiquette could be learned. Christmastime brought some of the most elegant decorations and a very special atmosphere. Children could write a letter to Santa and mail it in the Santa mailbox. And of course, many shoppers remember the elegant silver tissue–lined gift boxes with ribbon. They even had a program where models would walk around showing various styles to customers, including a back-to-school show where teenagers put on a fashion show as they introduced the newest fashions. In 1974, the Daly Bros. Furniture store was purchased down the street, and it became Jacobson's Store for the Home. Unfortunately, the company found itself in economic trouble in the 1990s. The Dearborn location was closed in 1997, and the company declared bankruptcy in 2002. The structures were torn down, and beginning in 2004, the former Jacobson's store site was used to build new condos, two new city-owned parking decks and a pair of Michigan Avenue buildings known as West Village Commons.

The number of quality stores that area residents have been able to peruse is truly astounding. For instance, Crowley's, Detroit's second-largest department store, decided that Dearborn was the perfect location to open its first branch store. The year was 1958. It served as the anchor store of the $5 million Westborn Shopping Center on the corner of Michigan Avenue and Outer Drive. The store was a tri-level design and contained over 106,000

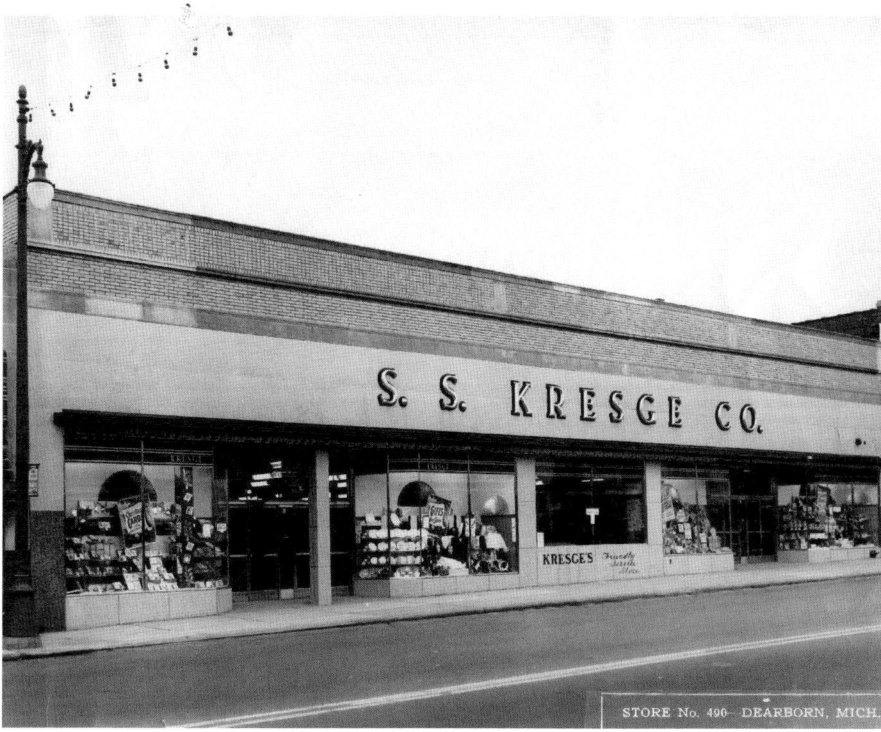

In 1928, one of the few remaining structures from the Detroit Arsenal, the saddler's shop, was torn down to make way for an S.S. Kresge store. Shown here in 1948, the five-and-dime operated at this location until 1973. *Dearborn Historical Museum.*

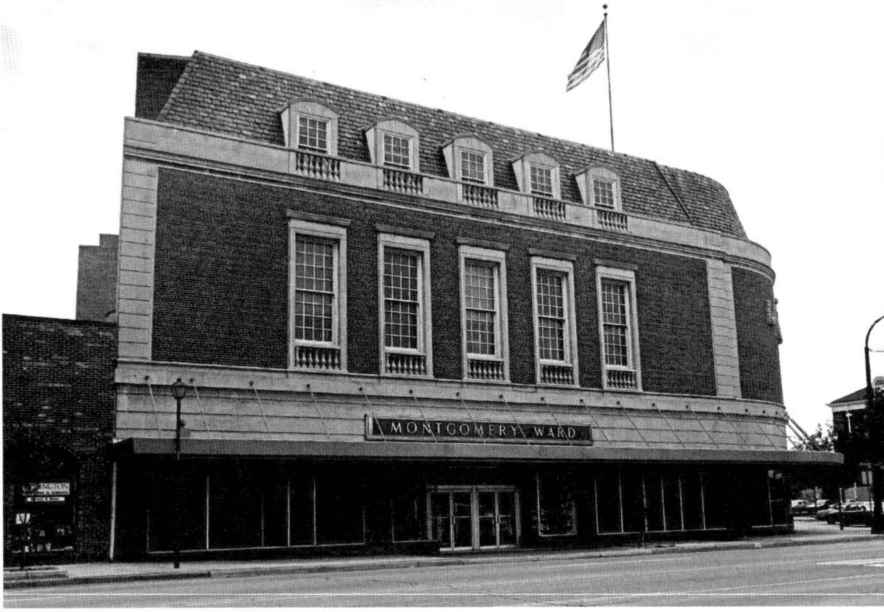

The Montgomery Ward location in Dearborn was at Michigan Avenue and Schaefer Road. The store opened in 1937 and, over the years, expanded to over ninety-three thousand square feet of shopping area. *Dearborn Historical Museum.*

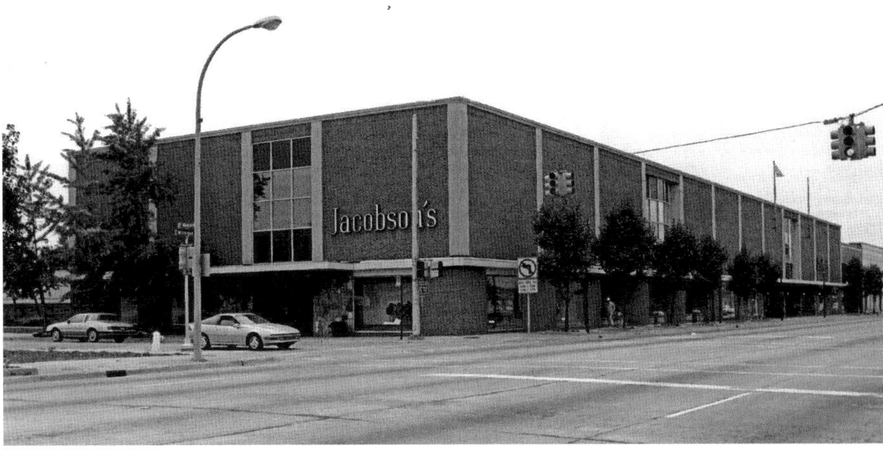

A premier store in the form of Jacobson's moved into Dearborn in 1964. The level of customer service was unparalleled in the area, and a visit to this store was a special experience. *Dearborn Historical Museum.*

square feet of floor space. One thing that patrons could always count on at Crowley's was a large selection of quality merchandise. The goal of the store was to provide the greatest variety possible in order to appeal to each shopper's particular taste and desire. The extensive training program the employees had to complete meant a better and smoother shopping experience for customers. The company was organized in Detroit in 1908, and management decided that the celebration of its fiftieth anniversary would be the perfect occasion to open the Dearborn location. The store thrived for years until the late 1990s, when new retail players cut into the store's market share and the purchase of an East Coast chain brought losses that were just too much to recover from. Many of the locations were sold off, and the Westborn store was demolished and a Kroger constructed on the property. A much-beloved store moved into history and now lives on as fond memories in the minds of the many shoppers who walked the aisles.

But no discussion of Dearborn retail would be complete without mentioning Muirhead's Department store. It was with hard work and dogged determination that John Muirhead was able to make the mark he did in his life, specifically in Dearborn. Muirhead came to the Detroit area at a very young age from the upper peninsula. He worked his way through law school and graduated from the Detroit College of Law. He was working as a practicing attorney in downtown Detroit when he met his wife and found a calling elsewhere. Muirhead purchased the corner lots at Michigan Avenue and Military Street and built his own independent gas station in 1938. While the station was successful, it was his wife, Alberta, who encouraged him to open up a toy store. The toy store, established in 1946, was another huge success, especially at Christmastime when Santa arrived. Children had a chance to ride a mini-train and then visit Santa in an igloo. The igloo was a perfect photo opportunity, as visitors could climb up in a sleigh, providing the perfect backdrop. Additions were made over the years, and eventually the shop became a location that offered much more than toys. Muirhead's included three levels of fashions as well as departments for the whole family. Patrons knew that if they bought any clothing items at Muirhead's, they were going to be walking around in style very soon. The store closed its doors in 1990 and was sold to Oakwood Healthcare Systems. It operates with a very different purpose today, but the building retains the Muirhead name in honor of two people who brought so much joy to children and parents alike. Both John and Alberta Muirhead became great examples of Dearbornites who not only possessed tremendous entrepreneurial spirit but also had the heart to give back to the community. In late 2007, Alberta

Muirhead gave a $500,000 gift to the Oakwood Healthcare Foundation to support nursing education. The contribution created the Muirhead Scholars Program in honor of John and Alberta Muirhead. This endowment fund assists the best and the brightest employees within the Oakwood Healthcare System in pursuing their advanced bachelor of science in nursing and master of science in nursing degrees. The full-ride scholarships are awarded annually to Oakwood employees. Though both are gone now, as is their store, the name Muirhead lives on in a truly meaningful way.

As Dearborn continued its tremendous growth into the 1960s, a variety of department and specialty stores were built to fulfill the needs of a diverse population. The People's Outfitting Company, located at 14225 Warren Avenue between Maple and Williamson Streets, was originally founded in Detroit in 1893 and immediately offered charge accounts with no interest, which was unheard of at the time. As the original store grew in popularity, new stores were built in the suburbs, including Dearborn. The Dearborn location opened in 1929. Mainly a furniture warehouse store, there were other items available as well. The press release put out by the company at the time of construction stated that "this structure incorporates practically every modern feature of warehouse design. It is of reinforced concrete construction and is fireproof throughout. It fronts 321 feet on Warren Avenue and extends 600 feet south along the railroad. By using a decorative face brick front, with shops along the entire Warren Avenue frontage, it has been possible to develop a beautiful exterior that will be a distinct credit to the community." The store occupied 18,000 square feet of the structure including a portion of the second floor. The company boasted that the operation would include "every modern labor-saving device, every comfort for our employees, every known aid to efficiency." The new warehouse included a 910-foot-long side with tracks running inside the building to help with service deliveries. Four of the largest known type of freight elevators at the time were installed to help speed up the operation. And there was also a garage which accommodated fifty huge delivery trucks. As a keepsake, for every purchase customers made, they received a silver horseshoe key chain with a penny in the middle of it. After many years of operation, Hudson's bought the building in 1959, and it became a Hudson's Warehouse. In 1985, the business was listed as a Hudson's Distribution Center. By 1998, Hollingsworth Logistics and other trucking-related concerns occupied the building.

In addition to the Hudson's location mentioned above, there were other Dearborn locations that existed. Founded in 1881 by Joseph L. Hudson in Detroit, the brand name thrived for decades and became one of the most

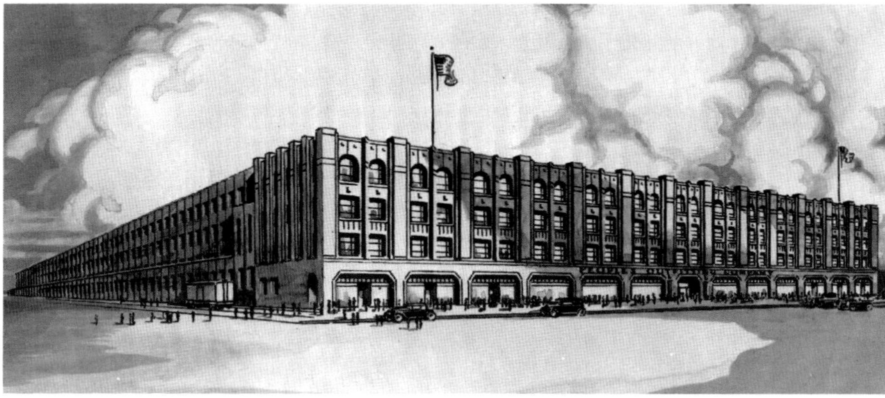

One of the earliest department stores in Dearborn, the People's Outfitting Company, was located at 14225 Warren Avenue. It opened in 1929 and operated until 1959, when it became a Hudson's Warehouse. *Dearborn Historical Museum.*

famous brands that this area has ever known. In 1963, a Hudson's Budget Store was built in East Dearborn on the southeast corner of Michigan Avenue and Greenfield Road. When Fairlane Town Center was built in 1976, the budget store moved into the basement of the J.L. Hudson's store, which became a hub of the mall. The evacuated building then became a K-Mart. Around 1995, the K-Mart closed. Farmer Jack then moved in for a short time, and now Kroger and ABC Warehouse occupy the site. After several years of declining sales, Hudson stores briefly became Marshall Fields, and then in 2006, all of the remaining stores were sold and incorporated into the Macy's chain.

The same year that the Hudson's Budget store opened, a Winkelman's began operations at 13520 Michigan Avenue. For much of the twentieth century, the name Winkelman's was synonymous with elegance and style at reasonable prices. In 1928, two brothers opened the first Winkelman's in Detroit. And over the next seventy years, over one hundred stores would be established. The concept from the very start was to develop a chain of stores in the suburbs. And this was before there was any discussion of suburban shopping centers. The philosophy behind the stores was the idea of giving the greatest degree of value and service for every dollar the customer would spend. And a huge part of making that philosophy work was to have personal contact between the merchant and the customer to the degree that a friendship had begun. After trying out a couple of different locations nearby, the store moved into the art deco John H. Schaefer Building. The store was known for implementing their philosophy to a very high degree. It closed in

1998, but the Schaefer building has been restored to its former glory and still attracts tenants. And Winkelman's is still celebrated and recognized as one of the nation's most recognizable and memorable stores.

When one analyzes the thread of retail history in the Dearborn area, one thing that becomes abundantly clear is that when a need or desire has arisen, there has always been someone who has found a way to step forward and supply the demand. Whether citizens were searching for food, clothing, eyewear, jewelry, farm implements, a bicycle or baked goods, those items were eventually available somewhere at some point. In earlier days, when Dearborn was still very much connected to farming, there were a lot of farming needs to be met, and the go-to place for many area residents was the Dearborn Feed Store. This store existed in many locations and ended up on the south side of Michigan Avenue down Mason Street. It began operations in 1926 at 117 Michigan Avenue. It moved to 1035 Mason (what would become Howell's Bar) in 1932. Then, sometime around 1940, the business moved to 1019 Mason and was owned and operated by William Frederick Krueger. The store order form advertised flour, feed, grain, hay and straw. It closed down in 1947 and the building was torn down. A Winkelman's was built on the location. When the need to hop on a two-wheeled contraption called a bicycle arose, it was time to head to Jack's Bike Shop. Started in 1935 and originally located at 1110 Mason Street, many Dearborn youngsters obtained their very first bicycle at Jack's. Those were the days of real customer service, when an attendant would come onto the showroom with a white apron on and pull out any bike a customer wanted to look at and adjust the seat for proper testing. Although the Mason location is long gone and closed in 1966, the Jack's location that opened in 1955 is still going strong at 24308 Michigan Avenue.

From large items to small, necessities to dreams, Dearbornites have always enjoyed perusing and purchasing items at stores from every category. And at any one time, Dearborn has had a little bit of everything in terms of retail. When there was a need for jewelry or corrective lenses, a local might find themselves in Lachman & Co. One of the oldest businesses in southeast Michigan, the business was started by a watchmaker in 1893, and the first location was in Detroit. A Dearborn location opened in 1941 at 4935 Schaefer Road. Over time, the business transitioned into trophies, awards and executive gifts, and one thing that customers could always count on was quality. The store closed in 1969, but the Lachman name continues on at a location in Southfield. The building is still standing but is presently vacant. The same year that

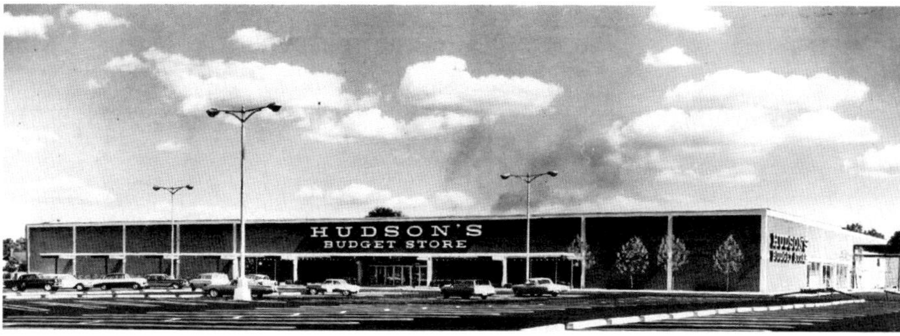

In 1963, a Hudson's Budget Store was built in East Dearborn on the southeast corner of Michigan Avenue and Greenfield Road. When the store moved out in 1976, the location became a K-Mart. *Dearborn Historical Museum.*

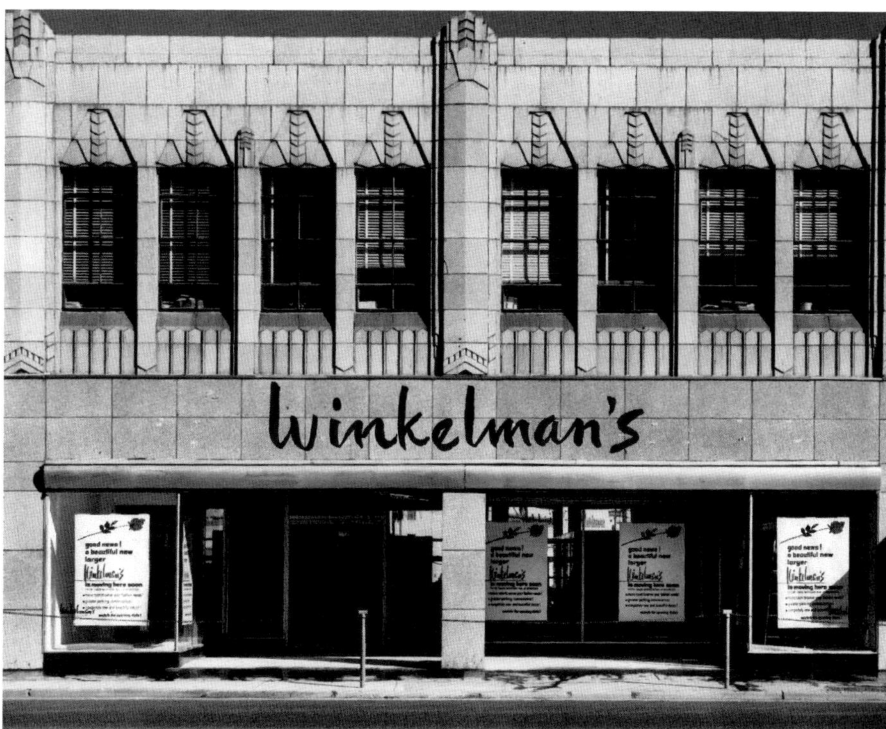

In 1963, Dearbornites experienced another stylish clothing store addition in the form of Winkleman's. After shuffling around to a couple of different locations, the store moved into the art deco John H. Schaefer Building. *Dearborn Historical Museum.*

Lachman & Co. opened, another jeweler came on the scene: Shifrin Jewelers opened a store in 1941 at 13710 Michigan Avenue. Founded in 1926 in Detroit, Shifrin quickly became known as a regional specialty retailer of fine jewelry, including a tremendous selection of diamonds, gold, precious and semiprecious jewelry and watches. The store became known as Shifrin-Willens in 1961, and in 1971, the business moved just down the street to the northwest corner of Michigan Avenue and Schaefer at 13600 Michigan Avenue. The jeweler closed in 1992. The original location housed at least two different podiatrists the year after Shifrin-Willens moved, and today, the building has a different face and is known as the Nagi Building, providing accounting and income tax services. The second location was torn down, and a Citizen's Bank stands on the site.

Generations of area shoppers will remember Adray Appliance on Carlyle Street. Established in 1955, there was a tremendous amount of variety on the shelves that appealed to different types of shoppers. For

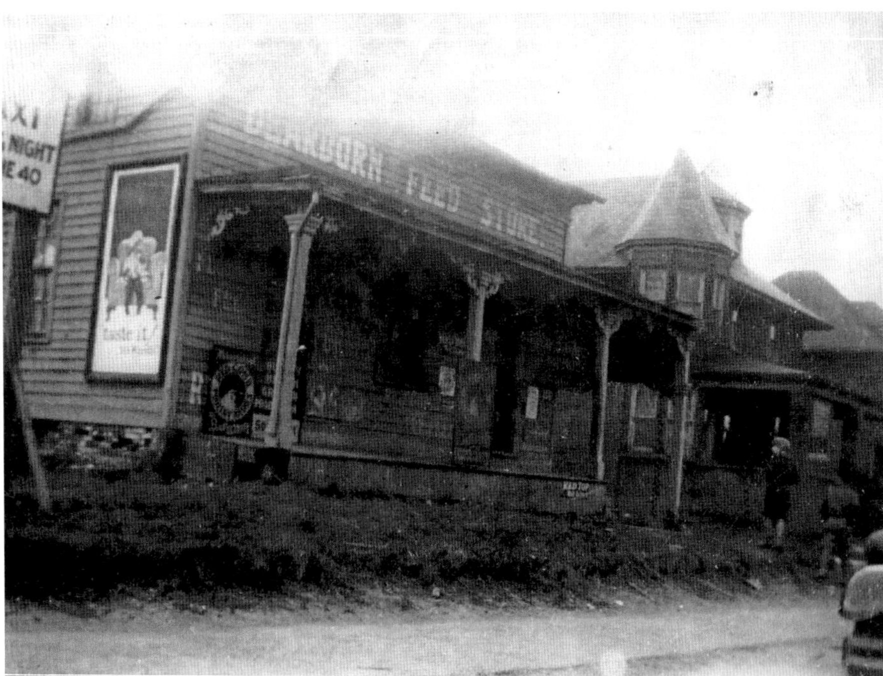

When Dearborn was still very much connected to farming, there were a lot of farming needs to be met, and the go-to place for many area residents was the Dearborn Feed Store, on the south side of Michigan Avenue on Mason Street. *Dearborn Historical Museum.*

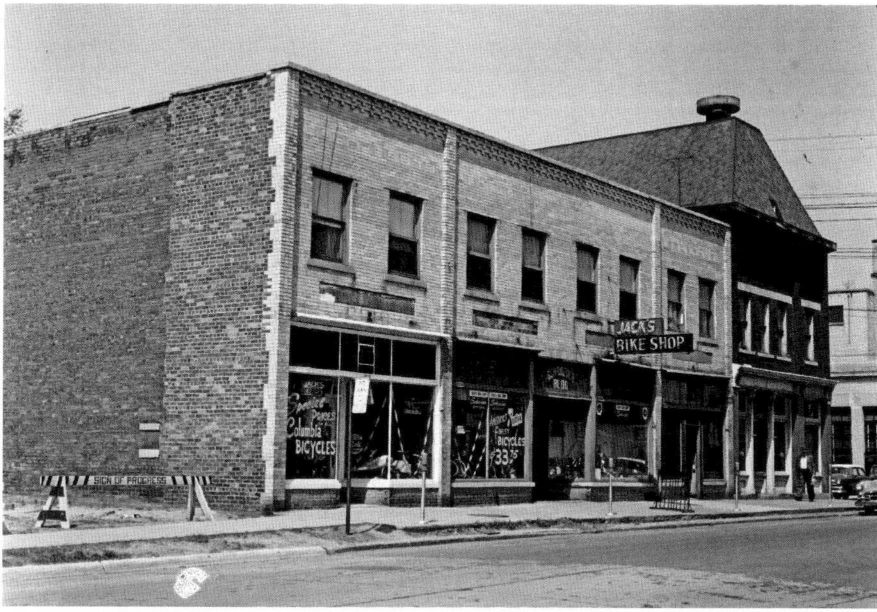

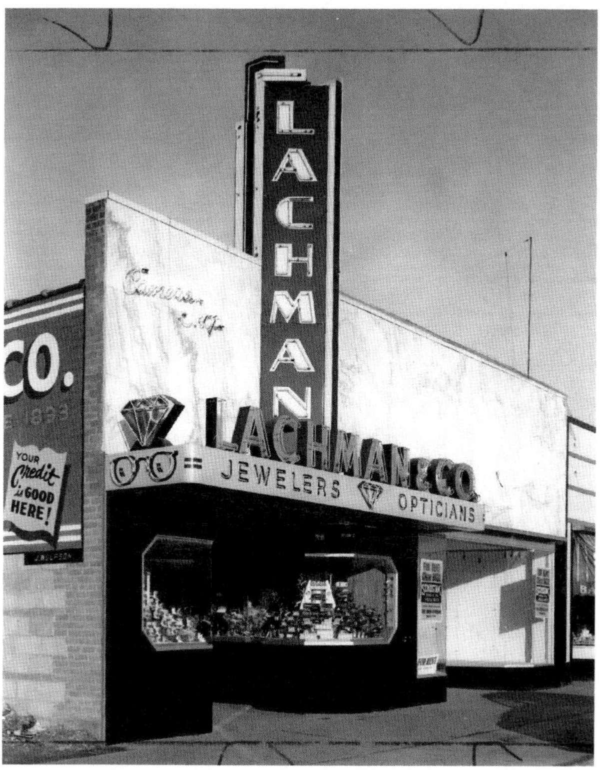

Above: Started in 1935 and located at 1110 Mason Street, many a Dearborn youngster obtained their very first bicycle at Jack's Bike Shop. The location is long gone, but Jack's is still going strong at 24308 Michigan Avenue. *Dearborn Historical Museum.*

Left: Lachman & Co. had been around since the 1800s, dealing in jewelry and corrective lenses, when the company decided to open a Dearborn location at 4935 Schaefer in 1941. The store closed in 1969. *Dearborn Historical Museum.*

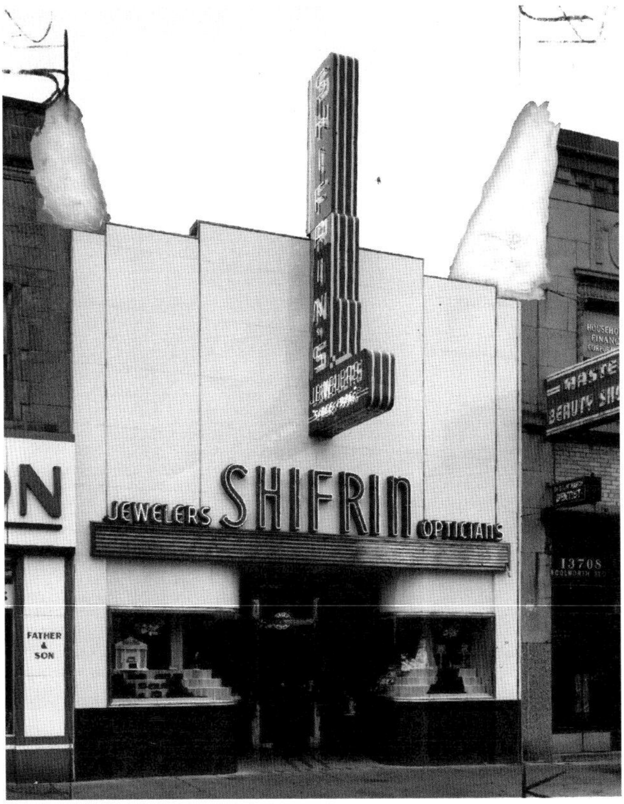

Left: Shifrin Jewelers opened a store in 1941 at 13710 Michigan Avenue. Fine jewelry was what it quickly became known for, and in 1961, the retailer became known as Shifrin-Willens. *Dearborn Historical Museum.*

Below: For those looking for work clothes or footwear, R. Price Workingmen's Store was the place to be. Established in the 1930s at 22074 Michigan Avenue, it offered Carhartt, which was a popular brand even back then. *Dearborn Historical Museum.*

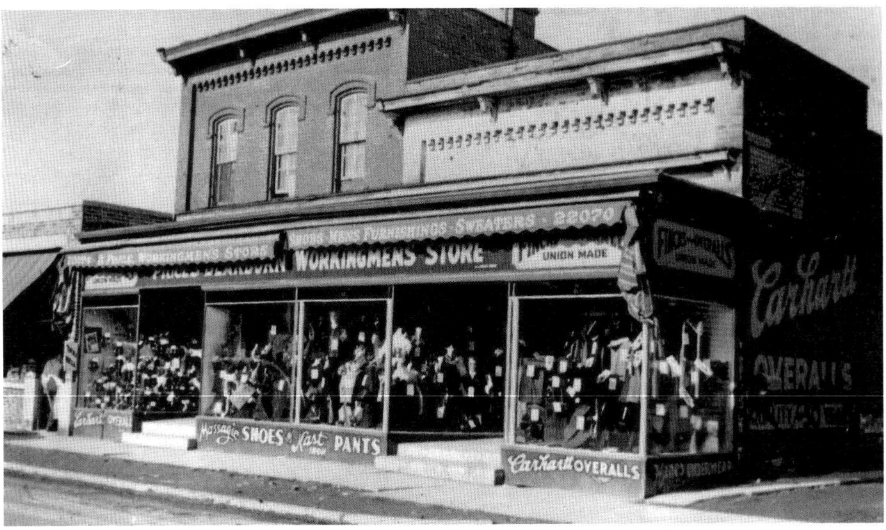

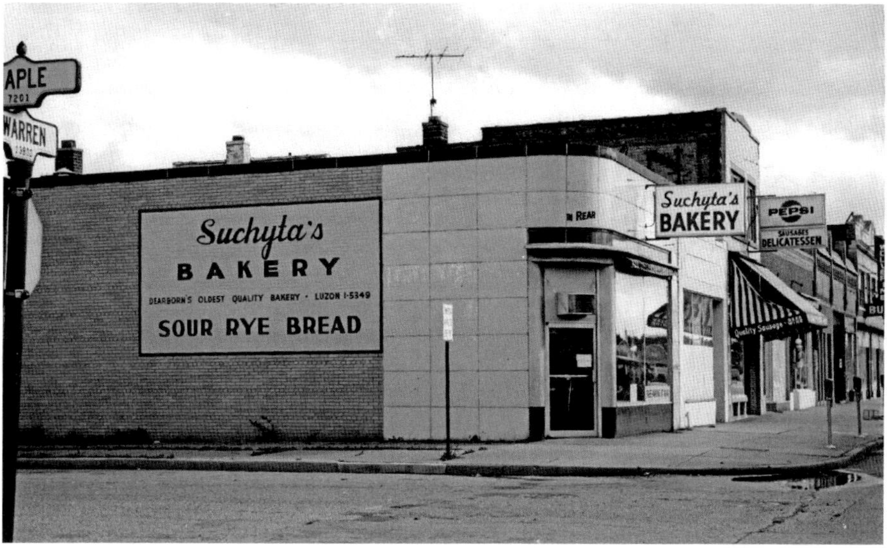

Suchyta's Bakery quickly gained a reputation for the best eclairs for miles around. One of the many locations was at 13750 Warren, pictured here in 1968. *Dearborn Historical Museum.*

years, Adray was known for supporting the community, including funding many different recreational activities—baseball and an ice arena—that bear the Adray name. Known for quality appliances and electronics, Adray was also a place where professional and amateur photographers could find anything and everything they were in need of. And the sales staff had a high level of knowledge and expertise in terms of the product lines carried in the store. The business was closed in 2009, and the building has remained dormant and for sale until the present day.

No matter what era, there will always be a need for work clothes, and R. Price Workingmen's Store was the perfect place to visit in order to purchase some Carhartt overalls or work boots. Located at 22074 Michigan Avenue in the 1930s, the business moved to 22263 Michigan Avenue around 1953. The store was damaged by fire the next year and closed. Price's Mens Wear moved into the location and thrived for many years. In 2003–4, Price's fought condemnation by the city and eventually moved out. The structure was torn down, and today, Bar Louie sits on the site. Sims Men's and Boy's Clothing opened up at 22074 Michigan Avenue in 1956 and closed in 1996. The building was torn down, and Ohm Spa now operates on that site.

Last but certainly not least, every city needs a place where residents can purchase some amazing baked goods, and Dearborn has certainly had its share of quality bakeries through the years. Suchyta's Bakery earned a place in the hearts and minds of locals, as the eclairs it served up are still raved about today. One of the many locations was at 13750 Warren Avenue, and the bakery quickly gained a reputation for some of the best baked goods one could find and top-notch customer service. The Warren Avenue location closed in 1988, and Golden Bakery occupied the building until 1998. Today, it is the location of Dearborn Halal Meat Market.

7
THE SIGN SAYS OUT OF BUSINESS

There are numerous elements that must coexist in a community for life to thrive. First and foremost, there must be hardworking citizens who have a desire to build something that will benefit the individual and the whole. In addition, businesses and producers provide the much-needed lifeblood that is essential in creating and sustaining a successful and sustainable lifestyle. From the days of the building of the Detroit Arsenal at Dearbornville, when there was a major call for brick makers, Dearborn has been home to a wide array of employers. Some of the names are famous and still going strong, like Ford Motor Company. But there are many smaller operations that came on the scene, flourished for a while and were gone. But either way, they are part of the fabric of what we today call Dearborn, and they provided what they could while they existed here.

Some of the names of past businesses are much more recognizable than others. In the case of the Kandt Lumber Company, many who are familiar with Dearborn or who grew up here will recognize that name, as Charles Kandt served in a number of roles in the community. He opened a hotel in 1903 and had a hardware store on Michigan Avenue where farm implements and tools were sold. He also served on the city council and as a member of the chamber of commerce. Then, in the early 1920s, he formed the C.A. Kandt Lumber Company, originally located at 23785 Michigan Avenue. Wood has always been a necessary and desirable building material, especially in the days when new neighborhoods were being built. And Kandt quickly gained a reputation for quality and service. Customers could bring their plans to the lumberyard, and employees would cut every piece needed to perfection and make sure everything fit together. It was the only place in the city where you could get wonderful hardwoods like cherry, walnut and oak without a special order. In 1953, there was a major fire on the grounds of the lumberyard, and the event caused a total loss. The heat became so intense that the wall on the block office building across the parking lot blistered. The fire department determined that the cause of the blaze was a shorted-out cord on a saw. The company continued on and moved just a short distance—right across the street to 23717 Kean. Operations continued until 1976, when everything was shut down. Today, that entire area is mainly occupied by the Village Ford complex. One of the structures remains that had survived the fire. The building was converted and is today Liberty Automotive.

Another lumber company operating just prior to the Kandt Lumber Company was formed was the S.D. Lapham Lumber Company. The Laphams were one of the pioneering families in the area and owned and operated a one-hundred-acre farm on what is today the corner of Military Street and Monroe Street. Samuel Lapham was involved in numerous enterprises, including helping his father in establishing Dearborn's first bank in 1896 and operating a general store and a butcher shop. He also served as president of the Village of Dearborn. The lumber company was located between Michigan Avenue and the Michigan Central Railroad, close to Howard Street. The address was 22167 Michigan Avenue. The business was in operation from 1911 to 1918, when it was sold to the Ternes & Guinan Lumber Company. By 1955, the Ternes & Guinan Company had become Ternes Supply Company and transitioned into largely selling paint. This new iteration moved to 1150 Mason Street in 1987. It is uncertain when the building that housed the lumber companies came down.

In an era before automobiles took center stage, there was a need for horse-related merchandise. And into that void stepped Herman Blankertz. In 1880, Blankertz and his new bride settled in the village of Dearborn. They found such a housing shortage that they moved into what had been the arsenal office just west of the commandant's quarters. It wasn't long before Blankertz set up a harness shop inside of the three-bedroom structure. This was a natural transition, as he had served in the U.S. Army as a saddler. He also served the area as a fire chief and village treasurer and on the school board and village council. His son Walter is infamous for having been the only person from Dearborn who died in World War I. In the early 1900s, what had now become a home and harness shop was torn down to extend Monroe Street north from Michigan Avenue. Blankertz then set up operations in what had

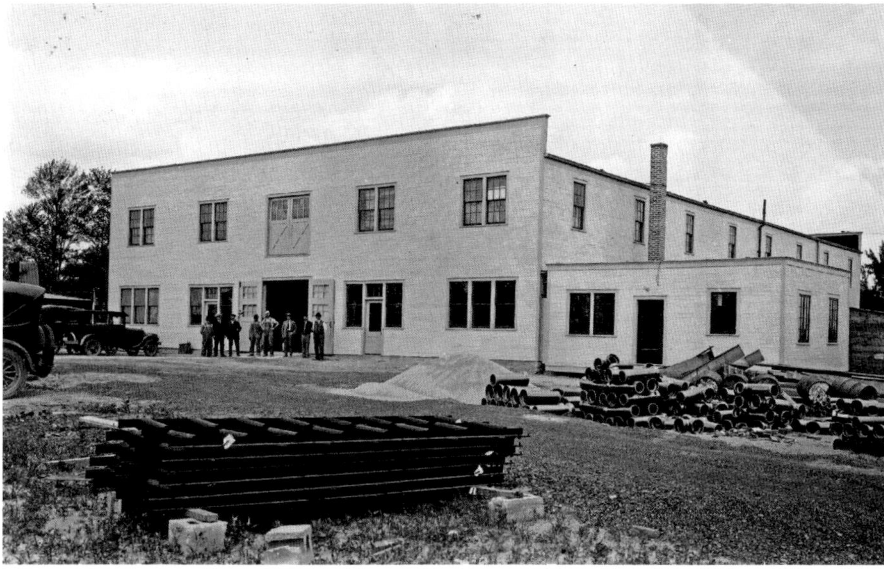

The C.A. Kandt Lumber Company was established in the early 1920s at 23785 Michigan Avenue. When a fire destroyed the business in 1953, the company moved across the street and continued until 1976. *Dearborn Historical Museum.*

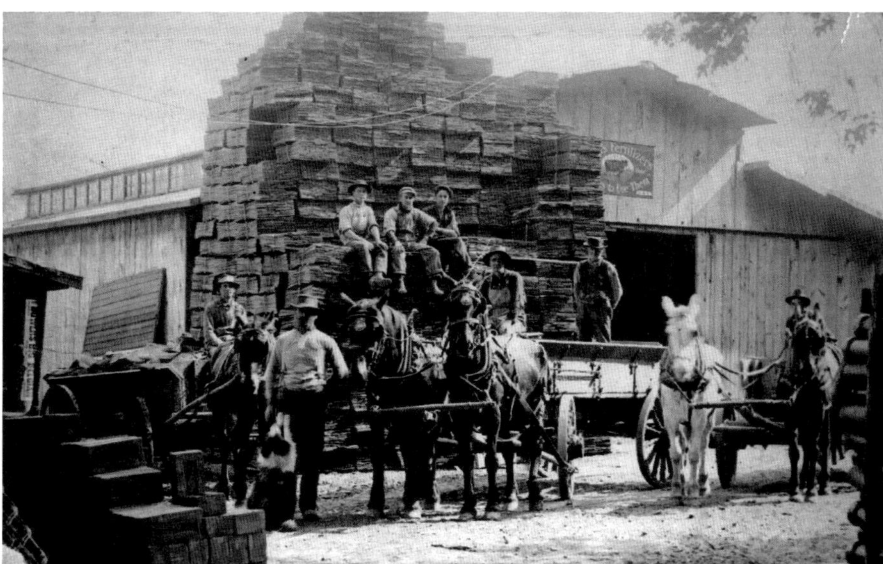

Any growing area will have a need for lumber and various woodworking skills. The S.D. Lapham Lumber Company filled this great need in the early 1900s at 22167 Michigan Avenue. *Dearborn Historical Museum.*

been an old feed shop building and moved it to 22064 Michigan Avenue, just a few feet west of where he had been. The new location now rested between Monroe Street and Mason Street. He closed up shop in 1925. The structure bore the name White's Beauty Shop during the 1930s, and the building was torn down in the early 1940s.

A business uniquely connected to a specific time period was barrel making. What today has mainly become associated with the storage of wine, whiskey and craft beer, a century ago and more, barrels were made to store everything from non-liquid substances such as flour, sugar, pickles or fish to a variety of liquids. Barrel making required the construction of hoops and staves. In 1905, the Marks brothers set up shop right at the foot of Morley Court by the Rouge River and commenced producing hoops and staves until 1907, when they moved their operations to Mount Clemens. No trace can be found of the shop when analyzing the aerial images that were taken of the area in 1925.

Concrete has long been used in various types of construction. The first commercially successful concrete block machine was invented in 1900, and soon, the concrete block became widely used during the first half of the twentieth century. In many structures, the concrete block composed

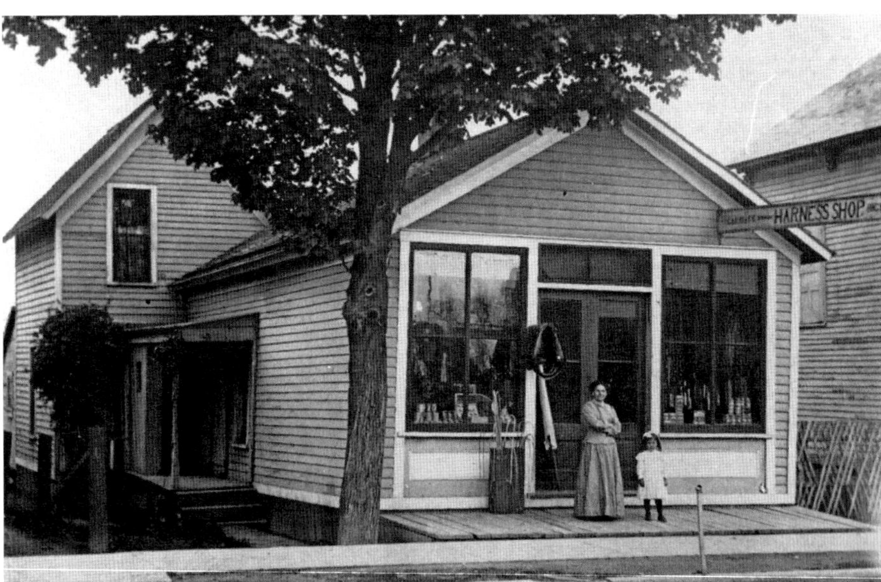

Herman Blankertz set up a harness shop in an old feed shop building and then moved the building to 22064 Michigan Avenue, just west of Monroe. *Dearborn Historical Museum.*

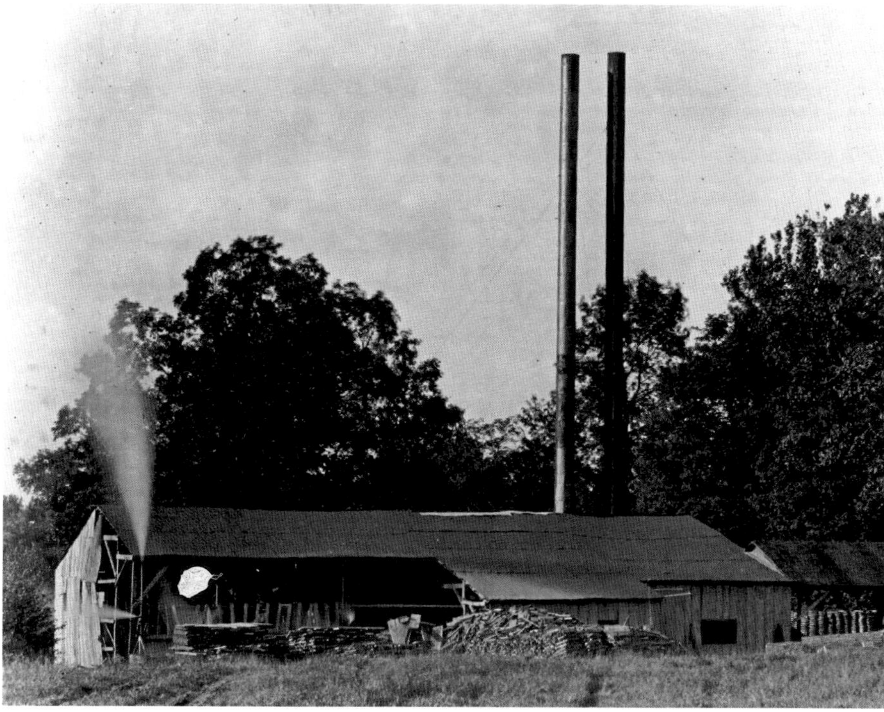

In 1905, the Marks brothers set up shop right at the foot of Morley Court by the Rouge River and commenced producing hoops and staves for barrels until 1907. *Dearborn Historical Museum.*

columns and was used for load-bearing walls. Many houses began to employ a concrete foundation. The first cement block plant in Dearborn was owned and operated by Floyd Maxwell and his father, Frank. The plant was started in 1904 and was located on Garrison Street between Oakwood Boulevard and Brady Street. The partially hollow construction blocks were made of gravel, sand, cement and water. The first house in Dearborn made with these concrete blocks was built in 1905 and was occupied by the Binkley family at what is now 21565 Garrison Street. With the death of Frank Maxwell, the plant closed down in 1910. In the 1920s, there were two concrete block companies that had picked up the mantle from the Maxwells: Frink at 126 South Mason Street and Dearborn Concrete at Oakwood Boulevard and Mechanic Street.

One of the most fascinating institutions to ever operate in Dearborn was known as St. Joseph's Retreat. The Retreat was a four-hundred-bed hospital for the mentally ill. It was built in 1885 by the Daughters

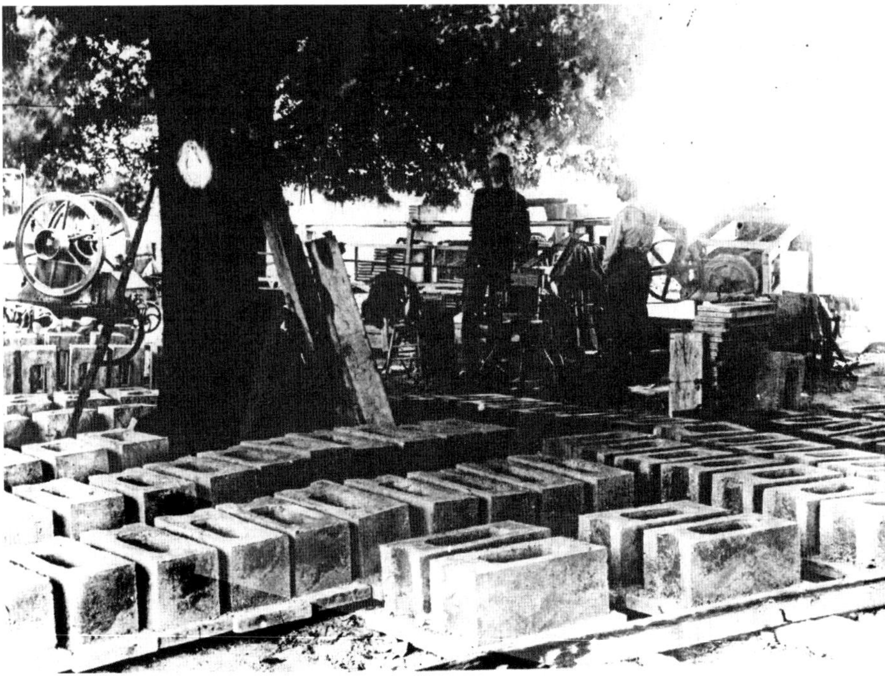

The first cement block plant in Dearborn was owned and operated by Floyd Maxwell and his father, Frank. Operations began in 1904 on Garrison between Oakwood and Brady Streets. *Dearborn Historical Museum.*

of Charity of St. Vincent De Paul on 140 acres on the northeast corner of Michigan Avenue and Outer Drive. The hospital was the first private mental facility in Michigan. The first patients were Civil War veterans, and later, alcoholics and drug addicts were admitted. Other patients with curable conditions were treated at the institution as well. The interior décor was of a rich quality and created a welcoming environment. There was even an amusement hall where the patients would participate in plays, tea parties, games and billiards and listen to music. Time and wear took a toll on the structure, and after new types of treatments emerged, it was decided that the facility had become obsolete. In 1962, the retreat was closed and the impressive complex torn down.

The word *engineering* has long been associated with Dearborn, especially because of the role Henry Ford and Ford Motor Company played in the area. However, Dearborn has had its fair share of manufacturing- and engineering-related companies. One such company that many readers might not remember made a true splash in its area of expertise. The Traffic

Transport Engineering Inc. was located at 14301 Schaden (Prospect) near Schaefer. Founded in 1944, it was the largest producer of automobile transport trailers by 1952, and the company produced trailers for every state in the union. Operations ceased in 1973, and the property was taken over by the Don Lee Liquor distributor. As of 1998, Tri County Beverage Company was at the address and had modernized the building. As of this writing, the building is vacant. Another huge success in its day was the Hexagon Tool and Engineering Corporation. Originally the Hexagon Tool and Die Company, which produced automotive and tractor parts, it was reorganized in 1940 in order to manufacture army ordnance items during World War II. Located at 23830 Harvard Street, the operation was presented with a meritorious award from the army for its production. After the war, it continued in business until 1987. For a time, Wholesale Bindery moved into the building, but it moved to Mount Clemens. As of the publishing of this book, the building is vacant.

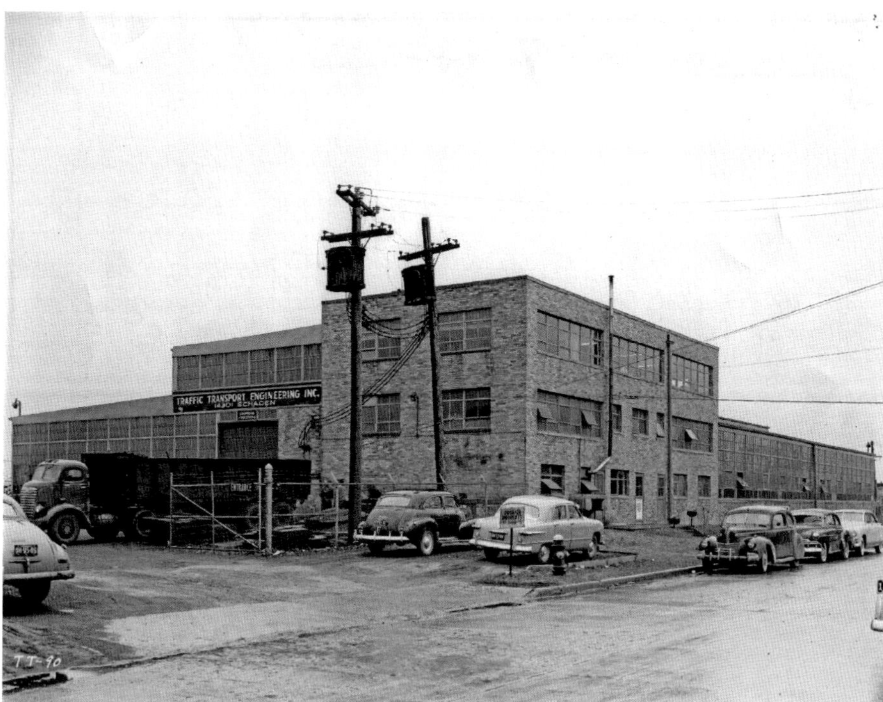

Traffic Transport Engineering Inc. was located at 14301 Schaden (Prospect) near Schaefer. Established in 1945, by 1952, it had become the largest producer of automobile transport trailers in the country. *Dearborn Historical Museum.*

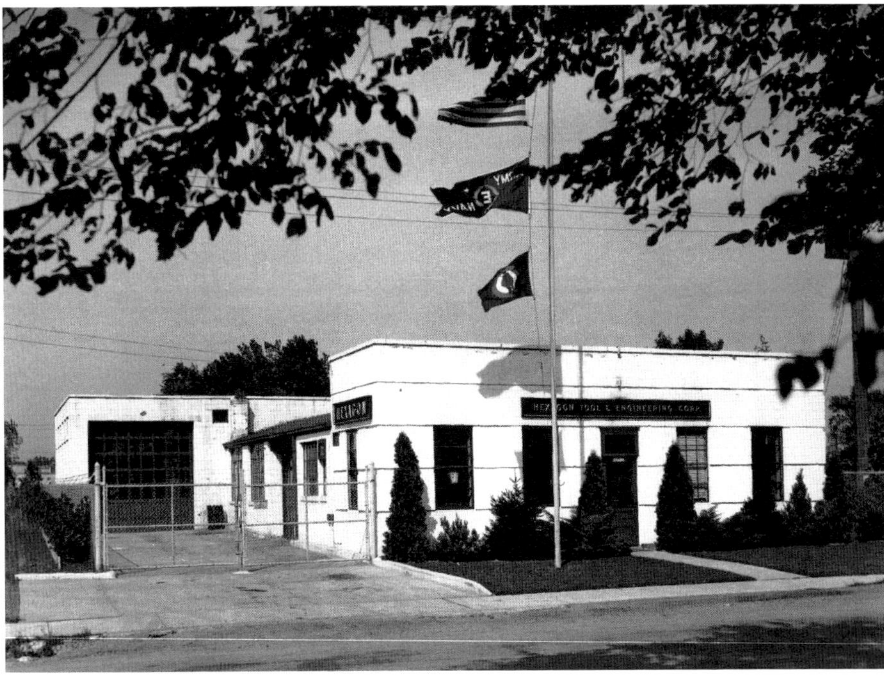

Located at 23830 Harvard, the Hexagon Tool and Die Company initially produced automotive and tractor parts but was reorganized in 1940 in order to manufacture army ordnance items during World War II. *Dearborn Historical Museum.*

While the automobile will forever be linked to Dearborn, there is another mode of transportation that the area has had a hand in advancing: aircraft. Henry Ford is not the only mechanically inclined person who has passed through or lived in Dearborn. William Bushnell Stout was a mechanical genius at a very early age. When he moved to Detroit in 1914, Stout was initially involved with automobiles, but because of World War I, he found himself redesigning a U.S. Army airplane. Stout caught the eye and ear of Henry Ford when Ford overheard him say that the area needed an airport and a plane factory. This was the beginning of a lifelong friendship between Ford and Stout. Ford and his son, Edsel, had long had an interest in the value of airplanes to the general public. Stout established the Stout Engineering Laboratories in Dearborn in 1919 and built the first American commercial monoplane. In 1922, the Stout Metal Airplane Company was formed with a promise to investors that their money would be contributing to aviation in the Detroit area. When the Ford Airport was built in 1924 with the encouragement of Stout, Ford purchased the Stout Metal Airplane

Company, which became a division of Ford Motor Company, and hired Stout to head it. A factory was built on the grounds of the Ford Airport, located off Oakwood Boulevard across from the Dearborn Inn. One of Stout's most notable achievements at the Ford Airport was the thick-winged Ford Tri-Motor, known as the "Tin Goose" because it was an all-metal plane. Stout worked on numerous aircraft and engines while here. Unfortunately, in 1926, a fire destroyed the Stout factory and all of the airplanes and engines in it. A new factory was built that consisted of two buildings with the largest doors in the world at the time. The Ford Tri-Motor was a tremendous success in the beginning, and Ford became the first company to use the moving assembly line to produce aircraft. As the Great Depression set in, sales of the Tri-Motor plummeted, and Stout left the company in 1933. Ford closed the aircraft design and production division in 1936. The only remnant of this era that still exists on the grounds of what is now the Ford Proving Grounds are the original aircraft hangars, which are used as part of the current Ford testing facilities.

Dearborn, while almost being synonymous with the name Ford, has had other automobile industry players within its borders. One of the more distinctive companies was called the Graham-Paige Motors Corporation. The Graham brothers had been involved in a number of different ventures in the early 1900s when they decided to give the passenger car business a try. They purchased a plant at 8505 West Warren Avenue near Wyoming that had produced vehicles under the name of Paige-Detroit. They changed the name of the company to the Graham-Paige Corporation. The million square feet of space allowed for some large production numbers. In 1929, over seventy-seven thousand units were produced. The model was a well-engineered and well-built car. With the onset of the Depression, the success of 1929 was not to be repeated, and production plummeted to thirteen thousand units in 1932. The company managed to stay afloat through the Depression years until the entry of the United States into World War II. During the war years, the plant was leased to Chrysler Corporation for the manufacture of bomber fuselages. In 1946, Chrysler purchased the plant from the Graham-Paige Motors Corporation and produced the DeSoto there from 1946 until 1958. For the next three years, production shifted to the luxurious Chrysler Imperial. In 1961, Chrysler sold the plant to investors. In later years, portions of the building housed Arlan's Department Store and Shatila Foods, which is connected to Shatila Bakery. Most of the building has stood vacant for many years, and it is in the process of being torn down as of the writing of this book.

BIBLIOGRAPHY

Bryan, Ford R. *Beyond the Model T: The Other Ventures of Henry Ford*. Detroit, MI: Wayne State University Press, 1997.

———. *The Fords of Dearborn: An Illustrated History*. Detroit, MI: Harlo Press, 1992.

———. *Henry's Attic*. Dearborn, MI: Ford R. Bryan, 1995.

Catton, Bruce. *Michigan: A History*. New York: W.W. Norton & Company Inc., 1984.

Dearborn: Fifty Years of Progress. Dearborn, MI: Dearborn Historical Museum, 1979.

The Detroit Arsenal Story: 1833–1875. Dearborn, MI: Dearborn Historical Commission, 1978.

Eaton, Eleanor. *Dearborn: A Pictorial History*. Virginia Beach, VA: Donning Company, 1984.

Hutchison, Craig E. *Dearborn, Michigan*. Charleston, SC: Arcadia Publishing, 2003.

Lewis, David L. *The Public Image of Henry Ford: An American Folk Hero and His Company*. Detroit, MI: Wayne State University Press, 1987.

Nowlin, William. *The Bark Covered House*. Dearborn, MI: Dearborn Historical Commission 1992.

School Sketches. Dearborn, MI: Dearborn Historical Commission, 1982.

Werling, Donn P. *Henry Ford: A Hearthside Perspective*. Warrendale, PA: Society of Automotive Engineers, 2000.

Articles

Arneson, Winfield H. "The Builders of Dearborn: Six Mile House Proprietor: John H. Schaefer." *Dearborn Historian* 29, no.1 (Winter 1989): 21–25.

———. "The Builders of Dearborn: The Ten Eyck Taverns Conrad Ten Eyck & Frank A. Gulley." *Dearborn Historian* 31, no. 4 (Autumn 1991): 107–9.

INDEX

E

F

G

H

I

J

K

L

W

ABOUT THE AUTHOR

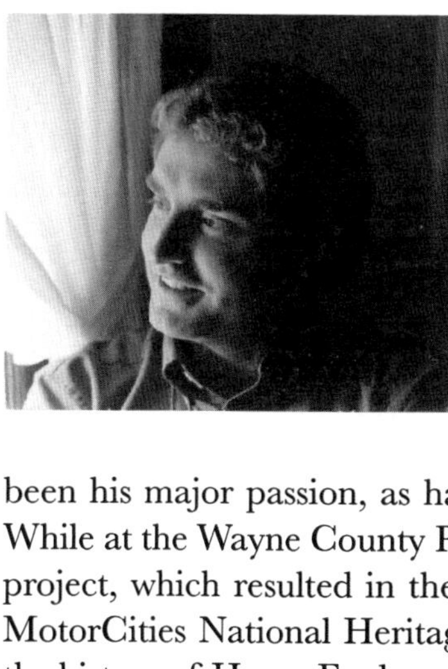

Craig Hutchison is a historian, researcher and author. He has worked in history-related positions for such institutions as the Henry Ford Estate, The Henry Ford, Wayne County Parks and the Dearborn Historical Museum. A lifelong resident of the hometown of Henry Ford, Dearborn, Michigan, Craig earned a BA in History at the University of Michigan. The study of history has always been his major passion, as has the opportunity to write and be published. While at the Wayne County Parks, he served on the National Heritage Area project, which resulted in the Detroit Metropolitan area being named the MotorCities National Heritage Area. Craig has never been far away from the history of Henry Ford, and while at the Henry Ford Estate, he worked on projects related to the interpretation of history, including the improvement of tours and reenactment activities. Working as a historical interpreter at Greenfield Village, guiding the public as to what life was really like in the past, provided an interesting perspective compared to writing about historical topics. The Dearborn Historical Museum opened up a whole new world to Craig as he served as communications specialist. Having a great desire to continue training in this amazing field, Craig is presently pursuing an MA in Public History from Arizona State University. But truly, there is no greater thrill for Craig than to be able to share fascinating history with the public via the publishing of the written word, and his hope is that his fourth book is not only informative but also provides some thrilling moments for readers.